PURPOSE
Over
POSSESSIONS

PURPOSE *over* POSSESSIONS

*Decluttering Your Life
So You Can Live on Purpose*

JENNIFER FORD BERRY

DEDICATION

This one is for you God.

Thank you for giving me a vision for this book.

Thank you for all that you have taught me during this process of writing.

Thank you for helping me live out my own purpose each and every day.

Please bless each person that reads this book and guide them to their own

unique purpose that is waiting for them.

TABLE OF CONTENTS

ACKNOWLEDGEMENTS

I would like to thank each of you that spent your money or your time on this book. It means the world to me that you would read my words.

Mom: thank you for being the first person to read the final draft of this book. Thank you for helping me with edits and giving me your feedback.

Cindi Dolan: thank you for also proofreading my final draft.

To my dear friend Erin Dressel: thank you for your friendship, support and belief in my ministry.

Laura Dudek: thank you for designing the cover of this book and for being a constant source of support and prayer for me!

Kim Waggoner and Jessica Barone: thank you for being my number one cheerleaders throughout this process.

To my Thursday bible study ladies who worked through this entire book as a weekly bible study with me: your love, support and prayer mean the world to me.

To all of my clients that have allowed me into your homes: thank you. You have better equipped me for sharing this knowledge with the world.

To my children, Randsley Alexis and Bryceton Richard. I pray that you always have the courage to be your authentic self. I want you to know that God created each of you with a very specific purpose in mind before Dad and I even met you! I will always encourage and support you in pursuing that purpose with everything you have.

Finally, a very special thank you to my husband Josh for providing our family with the stability that allows me to pursue my own passions and purpose each and every single day. I love you even more for always believing in me.

INTRODUCTION

Do you feel overwhelmed because of everything that you need to get done in a day? Are you exhausted from trying to take care of all the stuff that you have accumulated in your life? Do you lack fulfillment? Do you feel stuck?

If so, you are not alone. I have met with hundreds of people just like you over the years, and I am here to tell you that there is another way, a better way to go through this life. If you are finding that you have less and less time and energy to spend on the things you enjoy doing, chances are you need to make a change. God did not create you so that you could work to gain more possessions and then be a slave to them. He does not want you to feel overwhelmed and stressed out. He wants you to have abundance in joy, peace and love.

Our society has been told over and over that more possessions or better possessions will make us happier, healthier, or more successful, and it's simply not true. But we continue to keep trying to prove that it will work. We spend the majority of our life working so that we can earn money. Then we use the majority of that money to pay for a home and continuously fill it with stuff that is supposed to improve our lives in some way but leaves us still feeling empty.

Not only does this stuff provide less and less joy as time goes on, but we can also start to resent it. Why is that? Because everything we bring into our life costs us some amount of space, time, energy, money or all of the above! If you don't believe me look around your home and take note of the different tasks required for each item you own. Look at how much space you are giving up and how much money you are spending just on maintenance. Then ask yourself if these things still make you happy. I guarantee some do, but most don't.

This belief that stuff will make us happy has never been more prevalent than it is today. We live in a world where we are constantly viewing images of other people's lives and possessions. It is hard not to play the comparison game when you see a photo of someone next to their brand new car while wearing a gorgeous Chanel dress and Jimmy Choo stilettos! OK, maybe they are wearing a dress from Target and a pair of Steve Maddens, but the material things in the photo aren't what matter at all; it is how that photograph makes you feel about yourself.

Maybe you see that picture, and you imagine how much happier you would be if you had that car. It may even ignite a fire in you to work harder this week so that you can start saving for a car like that. Maybe a year later you have worked enough hours to afford that very same vehicle! The day you finally sit in the driver's seat, you know you have reached a higher level of success in the world's eye. You can hardly wait to show off the car to all of your friends. And it works for a while. That car brings you joy!

But how long does it last? A month? A year? Five years? Sooner or later that joy will dissipate, and you will be left dreaming of the next more elaborate vehicle. And on and on the cycle goes. The same scenario could be used to describe your feelings about your clothes, your furniture, even your home! You can spend your life trying to fill a void by accumulating stuff, but I can promise you that eventually, things will still leave you wanting more because you don't need more material things. What you need is more meaning, more fun, more experiences, and more purpose!

True wealth does not come from anything you can buy in this world. It comes directly from God's blessing and favor. True joy comes from giving, serving, and loving. True contentment comes from knowing that you are using your gifts and talents every single day to make this world a better place in some way that only you can do. True fulfillment comes from living out the specific purpose God has for you.

I want you to realize that you have a purpose assigned to your life, a divine God-given purpose that has nothing to do with what you own. This purpose is perfectly matched to your gifts, skills, and personality. It was what God had in mind for your life before you were even born. If you can figure out what your purpose is and start spending more time and effort on that and less on your stuff, you will be a much happier person! I can only imagine how different this world would be if more of us were committed to living out our unique purpose in alignment with God's will.

If you picked up this book, I have to guess that you are wondering what it looks like to choose your purpose over your possessions in the type of world we live in today. Well, I can tell you that it is a lifestyle choice, one that is filled with intention and free of clutter.

As a professional organizer for almost two decades, I have been in hundreds of homes. I have arrived at beautiful, immaculate homes full of every possession you can imagine only to meet another person that answers the door and begins to explain how overwhelmed they are. They are usually exhausted from trying to maintain all of their belongings, and they think that if I can organize it all for them, life will be so much better. To a certain extent, this is true. An organized home <u>will</u> make you happier, give you an energy boost, and save you lots of time. And trust me, I LOVE providing that service. In fact, I have written three other books called Organize Now! that provide step by step plans to get every area of your life and your home organized.

But each time we begin the process of getting organized, most people realize there is a more profound process going on inside their spirit. The process of letting go of that which does not serve us is a very empowering and liberating experience. Getting organized forces us to face each of the items we have brought into our homes. It makes us realize how much stuff we actually have and how much of that stuff we do not need or use. Somewhere in the process, people begin to realize that what they truly want is more freedom, more contentment, more time for things they love to do, and more space to breathe.

I love helping people get their closets and cabinets organized. But what I love even more is teaching people how to live with intention and purpose. Intention can help you define what is important. Purpose gives you a reason to stick with the process. When you have both of these, it is easier to remove everything that does not belong.

I have a gift for seeing potential in people and space. I have used the principals taught in this book to help transform hundreds of lives, including my own. I have lived out my own journey of choosing purpose over possessions over the past two decades.

As an organized person, I love a good plan and to be blatantly honest, I like to be in control. My original plan included moving to South Florida from Western New York for college, so that I could obtain a degree in Business and Marketing that would enable me to work in Corporate America and make a lot of money. Life in Palm Beach County was an eye opener for this small town girl! I was living "the dream," floating on yachts, riding in fancy sports cars, and meeting wealthy celebrities. It certainly appeared that stuff could make people VERY happy.

Shortly after graduation, I moved to Charlotte, NC, because of the booming job market. There I made it to Corporate America and had the paycheck I always wanted, but I still didn't feel fulfilled. Then plans shifted drastically. I was standing in the newsroom at Clear Channel Radio where I worked, on that unforgettable day, September 11, 2001. By then, I had married my high school sweetheart, Josh, and was pregnant with our first child. As we all watched those planes crash into the World Trade Center, I was horrified, and remember thinking I did not want to waste another minute in life. A few months later, I was laid off from that job due to cutbacks. I was an unemployed new mom. I knew I wanted to do more with my life. Sure, I still wanted to make money and have nice things, but I also wanted to wake up every morning and do something that mattered.

I had been volunteering at a transitional house for abused women in my neighborhood. Speaking with those broken women each week was the toughest thing I had ever done. But I could see potential in them, and I desperately wanted for them to believe there was a greater plan for their lives. Nothing fulfilled me more than those Wednesday night meetings. That experience made me realize I loved helping other women.

Strolling through a bookstore one day I picked up a book called *Do What You Love, The Money Will Follow: Discovering Your Right Livelihood*, by Marsha Sinetar. I'll be honest at first, I laughed thinking, "Yeah right. How am I going to do what I love and still make money??" I loved helping women, but I had no clue how that would earn me a paycheck.

Throughout the book, Marsha kept asking, "What are you passionate about?" I had to answer all of these questions about myself.[i] Each time I was honest with myself about my passion, the word "organizing" and "helping women" kept coming to the forefront of my mind. That was something that got me excited!

My earliest memories include organizing. I organized my Grandma's jewelry every time I was there. I organized my bedroom continuously. I loved every aspect of organizing: improving space, sorting, implementing categories, and most of all, the peace and joy I felt after I completed the work.

This passion was something that was placed inside of me long before I was born. I just hadn't realized it yet. The only thing that was stopping me from pursuing a career in organizing was the fact that I didn't think I could make enough money doing it. At the time, I only knew about two other professional organizers: Julie Morgenstern and Peter Walsh. I looked up to both of these people because they made a career out of something I loved to do! They were the pioneers for our industry. They were helping people organize long before HGTV, Hoarders, and Pinterest. Finally, I took a leap of faith and started organizing professionally.

I was organizing a couple of days a week, and at home, while my daughter slept, I started sending out a simple newsletter called "Free Weekly Organizing Tips." It was a simple, straightforward email that included one organizing tip each week. Little did I know that God had a plan for that silly newsletter…it would eventually become the basis for my first book: *Organize Now!: A Week-by-Week Guide to Simplify Your Space and Your Life*.

Thinking back on those early days, I can see how God was there all along leading me, guiding me, and encouraging me to keep going even though I had NO idea where this new plan was taking me. He knew what His purpose was for my life and how He would use me to help others.

When I started as an organizer, I still did not realize it would turn into a purpose. Over the years of helping people get organized, I realized that my purpose was not to create "Pinterest Perfect" homes. My purpose is to help others see what is most important and then help them build their home and their life around that. After all, God has made it so that we all enter and leave this earth empty-handed. You can continue to focus on accumulating things, but in the end, will that matter?

I shared my story with you because I want you to find yourself in it somewhere. When God breathed life into you, He breathed an idea that nobody else can do quite like you on the entire planet! Maybe you don't realize what that is right now, but I am telling you there have been clues along the way. I want to help you find out what that is and start living it out every single day.

I am passionate about teaching people to let go of the things they no longer love or use, and how to give them to the people that need those exact items! Did you know there is probably a woman's shelter in your community that could use those blankets in your hall closet that are collecting dust? And there are children nearby that would love the toys that have been sitting in your attic! I am not going to say that you should give everything away and become a minimalist. But I am going to encourage you to take a closer look at what you own and encourage you to share the things you no longer love or need.

I have broken this book up into ten primary principals. When applied to your life, you will begin to see huge results. This book will teach you how to recognize and eliminate the clutter that may be distracting you from your God-given purpose. Each chapter will give you a strategy to live with more intention. It will teach you how to let go of things that are cluttering up your home and your mind without feeling guilty.

If you picked up this book because you want to get excited

about life again, I am super excited for you because I know you are going to be transformed. There is an amazing plan waiting for you! I can't tell you that this book is going to have ALL the answers to your life-provoking questions. But I can tell you it will inspire you to dream bigger, guide you to recognize clutter in your life and teach you how to eliminate it piece by piece. You will learn how to gain more space, time, energy, and money in your life. Your mind will be opened up to new possibilities!

Life is short, and the clock is ticking my friend. God does not want you to waste another day. He needs you to step into the incredible plan He has set aside for your life. Maybe the purpose of your life is to:

- *raise kind, generous children*
- *start a service that improves the lives of others*
- *give your time to a nonprofit that is helping to eliminate sex trafficking*
- *host a Bible study in your home*
- *provide a safe environment for teens to gather*
- *write a book that will change the way our society thinks*
- *create art that brings people joy*
- *make music that inspires others to worship God*

No matter what your purpose is, I can tell you there is no greater feeling than waking up each day knowing that you are living up to your fullest potential and your greatest purpose. YOUR LIFE MATTERS! God intended each of us to be part of His divine plan.

Now is your chance to transform your life. You will not regret it. I once heard:

Your words create your thoughts,
your thoughts create your emotions,
your emotions create your actions,
your actions create your habits,
your habits create your character,
and your character creates your destination.

Isn't that powerful?! If you don't like where your life is right now, you need to backtrack through this list and start over. We all have the power to change our life and choose a new way in any given moment.

So go ahead, turn the page, and dive in. By the end of this book, I hope you have figured out what your purpose is and find the courage you need to live it unapologetically for the rest of your life. Remember, we do not leave a legacy from buying things. We leave a legacy by doing things!

CHAPTER 1: POSSIBILITIES

Jesus looked at them intently and said,
"Humanly speaking, it is impossible. But with God everything is possible."
Matthew 19:26

D o you believe that anything is possible in life? I mean truly believe it. Can you stop for a minute and wrap your head around that verse? "But with God everything is possible." He did not say some things! He said everything! This statement is not just for a celebrity, a preacher or your neighbor. This promise is for ALL of us. Each one of us, even when you don't fully grasp it. Even when you don't understand it. Even when you don't believe it.

Friends, I know that we can all have moments of unbelief in our lives. But, our disbelief never changes the promises of God. And may I also remind you that God cannot lie! So basically, it is up to us to get on board with these promises, this way of thinking, these possibilities for our life! Otherwise, when we miss the boat, we have nobody to blame but ourselves.

Are you like I once was, laughing at the thought that you can make money doing what you love? I know there are times in life when the possibility of a situation getting better is hard to believe. I get it! I don't know your story, but I am sure it has lead you to the opinions you currently have about this life.

If you do believe anything is possible, then I am giving you a huge high-five right now because that means you don't let heartache and disappointment steal your hope. Lord only knows the heartaches and frustrations you have endured until the time of reading these words. None of us can get through life without experiencing difficulties. Unfortunately, some of us seem to have to endure far greater suffering than others. But we can still choose to believe in possibilities especially, if you believe in God. Because with Him, all things are possible!

So right now I want you to put all of your hesitations aside for just a bit and imagine new possibilities. Close your eyes right now for about 5 minutes and then while taking some deep breaths, pray this simple prayer:

> *Lord,*
>
> *I ask that you give me a vision of all the possibilities for my life. Open my eyes in areas where I may be blind. Give me your wisdom and guidance. Help me to understand the life you had intended for me when you created me. Show me my life from your perspective, Lord. In Jesus's name I pray,*
>
> *Amen*

By faith, we understand that the entire universe was formed at God's command, that what we now see did not come from anything that can be seen.

Hebrews 11:3

A vision is a mental imagine of what the future could look like. When God created the universe, He imagined the possibilities in His mind. He created a specific vision, and then that vision became a reality. Isn't it amazing to think that the manifestation of God's imagination created everything we can now see with our physical eyes??

In Kris Vallotton's book: *Poverty, Riches and Wealth: Moving From A Life Of Lack into True Kingdom Abundance,* he writes: "There is something very powerful about your imagination. It is vision that shapes our lives and directs our destinies. What you imagine has a huge effect on who you are becoming. You are forming your outer world with your inner thoughts."[ii]

For you to come up with a vision for your life, you must first imagine your own possibilities. A synonym of the word "possibility" is "hope."[iii] Think of something you have always hoped for that hasn't happened yet. Now imagine the possibility of it happening:

- *What would your life look like?*
- *What would it change?*
- *Who could you help?*
- *What could it mean for the next generation of your family?*

Now take it a step farther and envision how you would feel if these things happened. How would you feel about yourself? Proud? Content? Excited? Joyful? Relieved?

OK, you are ready. Take a few minutes and write down your hopes and dreams. Start to pray over this list daily. Put your faith in God that it will come to pass in His perfect timing.

Without imaging all the possibilities for your life, you will never be able to create a vision for your life. I like to think of a vision as a painted picture in your mind. One that will depict what you want your life to be. The more detail in the picture, the better!

Your vision is your BIG WHY. It's a compelling reason why you want to do something. It gives you direction, and it is your desired future. Your vision includes what you believe in (your core values). Having a vision will not only teach you how to be intentional with your life, but it can also change the course of your life forever.

When was the last time you let yourself sit and daydream? Hopefully recently! But I have found that many people haven't spent much time daydreaming since they were a child.

I remember when I was a little girl, I loved to climb trees. Since the woods surrounded our home, I had an abundance of trees! I would sit up in those branches, away from everything, and dream. Not only was it incredibly peaceful, but I swear I could envision my dreams coming true as clearly as if I were watching a movie. It was so easy to do back then because I was less distracted than I am now. Plus, I gave myself time and permission to do it! I wasn't sitting in that tree thinking, "I better hurry up so I can get back to cleaning the house!"

It's true. As adults, we have less time and more responsibilities. But that doesn't mean we can't make time to daydream. As long as you are still breathing, you have work to do on this planet, and daydreaming will fill your mind with the possibilities!

Jennie Allen says, "We are called to dream, but we're afraid to. But because we are called, when we don't act on it, we become restless. Restless to find purpose, to make a difference in the world, to matter."[iv]

I highly encourage you to set aside some time to think about all the possibilities for your life. Just let your imagination run wild! Ask yourself questions like:

- *If you could do ANYTHING with your life, what would it be?*
- *What are you most passionate about?*
- *What do you love doing?*
- *When are you the most joyful?*
- *What have you always dreamed about doing?*
- *What are your gifts?*
- *What would you do if you knew you couldn't fail?*
- *What could you contribute to the world that would make you feel proud or excited?*
- *What kind of parent do you want to be?*
- *What do you want your home to feel like?*
- *What do you want more of?*
- *What do you want less of?*
- *How do you want to be remembered when you have left this earth?*

In Mark, chapter 9 of the Bible, there is a story about Jesus healing a demon-possessed boy. The father brings the boy to Jesus and asks for mercy on him. He asks if Jesus can help them. Jesus responds by saying "What do you mean if I can? Anything is possible if a person believes." The father instantly cries out, "I do believe but help me overcome my unbelief!"[v]

I have to admit, I feel so relieved when I read that verse because I, too, believe and yet still struggle with unbelief at times. Then I feel guilty for my disbelief! But guilt does not help me to keep going when times are tough.

When we start to struggle with these feelings of doubt, it is the exact time when we need to learn to stop and cry out to God, "Lord help me overcome my unbelief!" Friend, there are going to be days when you are super fired up about the possibilities for your life. But there will also be days on this journey toward a purpose that you will have doubts and that is OK! When it happens, know that God is waiting and willing to pour more faith onto you! Faith is a gift from God, and the more we rely on Him, the more it grows.

Are you afraid of leaping into new possibilities? Are you afraid of what people will think? Does it feel like it is taking forever for your dream to come true?

I get you! I felt like I was lost in limbo for about two years. I was not writing. I lost my vision. I couldn't even think clearly. I completely lost my creativity. One day I was in the store Hobby Lobby, and I picked up a framed quote, (I love quotes) that said "Things Are About To Get Really Good". I felt compelled to buy it for some reason. I took it home and put in on my bathroom windowsill where I could see it every day. I didn't know what was going to happen, but I knew God had shown me that sign to remind me to keep my hope and faith in Him. I read that sign SO many times. Some days when I felt discouraged or impatient, I would think, "I guess this sign wasn't God because nothing is happening." Other days, my faith would be stronger and I would read it with every ounce of hope I had.

Look beyond your current circumstances.

There are many seasons in life. For example, you may currently have small children that need you to be home with them so that you can avoid daycare expenses. This doesn't mean you have to leave them now, but soon there will be a season when they may be in school. I wrote my first published book when my youngest was napping, and my oldest was at pre-school! Seasons keep changing and life rolls along. You never know what the future might have in store for you!

Do not let other people's opinions direct your steps.

How many stories have you heard about successful people receiving 100 "no's" before they got one "yes"? It happens all the time! God gives us all different opinions, personalities, and dreams for a reason. And guess what... this makes it difficult for us all to be on the same page at the same time! So it is 100% OK if nobody else in the world completely understands your dream. In fact, what other people think of your dream has nothing to do with whether or not you should pursue it. The truth is, if God put a dream in your heart, it is tied to the purpose He has planned for you. That's all you need to know.

Stop worrying about your own limitations.

If you have a dream in your heart, and there is no way you can accomplish it entirely on your own, chances are it is from God. He wants you to rely on Him and He wants you to ask for His help. These God size dreams and possibilities are placed in our hearts so that we can be used to fulfill HIS goals, not our own. God has all the details already figured out. He just needs feet on the earth to make sure His work gets done. With God on your side, you do not need to fear your own limitations.

Vision comes before provision. What is provision? It means to supply with equipment, especially for a journey. You will need help and equipment for your journey here on earth, and God is the perfect one to help you with that.

> Write my answer plainly on tablets, so that a runner can carry the correct message to others. This vision is for a future time. It describes the end, and it will be fulfilled. If it seems slow in coming, wait patiently, for it will surely take place. It will not be delayed.
>
> Habakkuk 2: 2-3

When you get clear about the vision for your life, the Bible says to write it down and make it plain on paper. Then have faith! God will come alongside you and provide opportunities for that vision to come to pass in ways that you can not even imagine currently. That is how He works. God loves to blow our minds! Spend some time daydreaming and imagining the possibilities for your life.

Give yourself permission to spend time dreaming. Then when you have a clear picture in your mind, create a vision board or a visual journal (personally like the journal). Look at it and pray over it every single day and watch what happens. These possibilities will eventually become your realities!

Be intentional about teaching your mind to dream big.

Your mind controls your brain.[vi] So fill it with positive and joyful information. Such as audio messages, books, music, and affirmations that will keep you focused on a more significant potential for your future.

Play out the "What If's" in your mind:

- *What if you could earn a living doing what you love?*
- *What if you used your gifts to help others?*
- *What if you quit your current job to start that business?*
- *What if you asked someone you admire for a quick phone call or a conversation over coffee?*
- *What if you took a big step into your purpose today?*

Do not share big ideas with small minded people it's a waste of time.

People that always expect the worst have little hope in a brighter future. These people are not going to get you where you want to go. Limit your time with anyone that is a negative voice in your head and seek out people that will encourage you to reach for the stars!

Train your tongue!

I believe our thoughts create our future but our words declare it to the world! Words have tremendous power! Stop complaining and sabotaging your future by speaking negatively. Train yourself to speak positively about your life. "Death and life are in the power of the tongue." (Proverbs 18:21, NKJV)

CHAPTER 2: PURPOSE

But I have spared you for a purpose - to show you my power and to spread my fame throughout the earth.
Exodus 9:16

Notice in the quote above God doesn't say the purpose is to spread your fame. The purpose he has in store for you is part of the plan to spread HIS fame, HIS glory, HIS kingdom. He wants YOU to be part of His plan! How amazing and exciting is that?

It is super thrilling, until that annoying little devil-voice sweeps in and says, "Why would the God of the universe want to use you???" I know because that is exactly what I thought. And you know what? I still fight that nagging feeling sometimes. There have been plenty of days (this past year in fact, while I was starting a new ministry), that I heard that same defeating statement. I am not going to lie. Those days have been hard! I have questioned myself a million times and quite frankly, have wanted to give up. But, deep in my soul, I know God is building my tenacity and my ability to stick with Him through the tough times. So instead of quitting, I think, and truthfully, sometimes yell, "Not today Satan!" and I keep on trucking.

Thankfully, God has given me teachers, books, words, podcasts and so much more to remind me that God always chooses imperfect people to do his work. Why? Because we are ALL imperfect! It may appear that a person you see doing what you have always dreamed about doing, looks like she has it all together. But let me tell you, my friend, THEY DON'T! They just started with a dream, then worked really, really, really hard. If they were smart, they prayed and surrendered A LOT! I can promise you there are still moments when they think, "Who am I to be doing this?," especially if they are out working for God. The devil hates people like that!

Purpose is something you uncover. Whether you realize it or not, you are being guided toward your purpose every single day. But for you to see this, you must put on God's lens. This means paying attention to the little ways in which God is working in your life. God will use any means He can to align your path to the purpose He has intended for you.

When you know what your purpose is, you plan ahead and start each day with that in mind. Purpose shapes how you think, how you spend your time and how you do life. Your life purpose is not your job or your role (daughter/son, mother/father, etc.). Positions and roles are vehicles through which you deliver your purpose.

Your life's purpose comes from within. It was planted inside of you as part of God's plan for His Kingdom before you were even born! It is your big "WHY?!"

In John Maxwell's book, *Put Your Dreams To The Test*, he says, "In my effort to clarify my dream, I discovered that the more clearly I saw my dream, the more clearly I was able to see my purpose. This is true, I believe, because a person's dream and purpose are intertwined. God designs us to want to do what we are most capable of doing."[vii] I believe this because He had our purpose intended for us before we were even born. He formed us in our mother's womb with the exact personality, set of gifts, insights, and talents we would need to see our purpose through. His plan was perfect; we have just lost our focus due to all the distractions in our way.

Friends, I want to tell you that there is no more excellent feeling in the entire universe than waking up each day knowing you are living your God-given purpose. Not only does it allow you to share your God implanted gifts and talents, but when you are truly aligned with God's will for your life, your purpose will help other people. Deep down, who doesn't want to help make the world a better place? Not to mention that this is the number one reason why people are remembered after they leave this Earth: not for what they had, but for what they did! I know it sounds cliche, but deciding how you want to be remembered and then working backward is a great way to live!

Consistent study of God's word is vital for staying on course to your purpose. I highly recommend that you commit right now to how much time you will give to spending in God's word each day. Not only will it give you the wisdom and insight you need for pursuing your purpose, but it will help you stay on course when the journey gets bumpy. It will help you handle stressful situations and lift you when you are down.

What if you currently have no freaking idea what your purpose is? First of all, you are not alone in thinking this. Each person comes to the realization of their purpose in different ways and in different amounts of time. Shortly I will give you some action steps that may speed up this process, but in the meantime, know that your purpose will have something to do with serving others and making a positive impact in this world. It will be something that God needs you to do for Him.

Later in his book, John Maxwell goes on to say "Everyone faces difficulty when working toward a dream. And if someone fails, he can make excuses for what went wrong, how the unexpected happened, how someone let him down, how circumstances worked against him. But the reality is that the external things do not stop people. It's what happens to them on the inside. Most people stop themselves from reaching their potential. They can pretend that people, things, and situations outside themselves are to blame for their failures, but in reality, they are to blame".

Even if you can not see your purpose clearly now, do not assume you don't have one. Every person on this Earth was birthed out of purpose. EVERY single one and that includes you. This truth is not just for the people that are already living out their mission. It is not just for the famous people you watch on social media doing what you dream of doing. IT IS FOR YOU. God NEEDS you to carry out the plans He has in store for you. If you don't fulfill your specific purpose, who will?

Rich was not only addicted to drugs, he was a drug dealer. His family was devastated and worried about him. His brother constantly brought the Word to him but Rich didn't give it much attention. His mom kept praying. Years went by until one day his choices started dragging him into a downhill slope. He was on the edge of losing his home, his wife and his family. He decided to finally check himself into rehab. That night he hit his knees and prayed to God to save him. By the morning his drug addiction was completely wiped clean from his body with no withdrawals! One day he noticed a bunch of neighborhood kids hanging out in this driveway. He started chatting with them. At the time Rich had no idea what God's purpose was for his life. The driveway chats lead to Rich and his wife, Jessica, taking these kids on a camping trip. Fast forward to today Rich is now a pastor with his own church and a growing youth ministry that picks kids up off the streets every Saturday night, feeds them, gives them a message and worship and then delivers them home. See God had a divine purpose for Rich's life all along but until Rich could clear the clutter caused by addiction he could not experience it. He was lost and broken...but God.

"And the Holy Spirit helps us in our weakness. For example, we don't know what God wants us to pray for. But the Holy Spirit prays for us with groanings that cannot be expressed in words. And the Father who knows all hearts knows what the Spirit is saying, for the Spirit pleads for us believers in harmony with God's own will. And we know that God causes everything to work together for the good of those who love God and are called according to his purpose for them. For God knew His people in advance, and He chose them to become like His Son so that His Son would be the firstborn among many brothers and sisters." (Romans 8: 26-29)

You don't have to say the perfect prayers or understand everything. You just have to start with a simple statement: "Lord I ask that your will be done in my life." If you say that prayer every day, I promise you cannot go wrong.

Put your trust in God because He works EVERYTHING for your good. That doesn't mean we get a perfect life; evil is still working against Him. But He can even use that. Note that God is not working to necessarily make you HAPPY all the time, He is trying to fulfill HIS purpose through you. That is why He brought you to this Earth, in hopes that you would achieve that purpose before He brings you back to Him.

So are YOU ready to find and conquer your purpose? I am so excited for you! Here are some steps that you will find helpful when trying to figure out what your purpose is or pursuing one that God has placed on your heart.

1. Daydream

As I mentioned in the previous chapter, we all need a little more daydreaming in our life. Stop right now and close your eyes for five minutes and imagine if you could spend more time doing something. What would it be?

2. Spend Time With God

I truly believe that God has all the answers for us and if we spend some time with Him, we would uncover our purpose. Time in the Word, time in prayer and time just listening for the voice of God can really make a difference if you are searching for your purpose. "You can make plans, but the Lord's purpose will prevail." (Proverbs 19:21)

3. Read, Read and Read Some More

It is incredible how you can learn anything in the world just by reading. I am a HUGE reader. I am always in the middle of 1-3 books at a time. I have kept a list of books on my computer that I have read (including a 1-5 rating) for years. Why do I rate them you ask? Well, it helps me remember what authors I enjoyed when I need a new book. These days, I mostly read non-fiction because I am in a learn, learn, learn frame of mind!

4. Think of Podcasts and Videos as Your Continuing Ed

We are blessed to live during a time when we can learn how to do almost anything in the world with a click of a button (that button being Google). My advice is to take advantage of this. I listen to podcasts or videos almost every single day. They are a great way to get an insight peek at how others are living and how they've succeeded which is excellent for inspiration. For example, on my podcast: *The 29 Minute Mom*, guests share inspiration, motivation, and education that will help moms live their best life.[ix]

5. Ask Those Closest To You What You Are Good At

Sometimes others recognize our gifts even before we do. Ask others what they think you are good at. Ask them if they have learned something from you or how you have helped them in the past.

6. Get Out and Try New Things!

It is hard to know what you are truly passionate about if you don't try new things. Decide what you want to try and then go do it. Maybe you can sign up for a new class on the topic. If you don't like it, try something else. Then do it again and again and again. The power of life is in your decisions, not in your condition. You get to decide; you get to choose the life you want to have!

CHAPTER 3: POSSESSIONS

Don't store up treasures here on earth, where moths eat them and rust destroys them, and where thieves break in and steal. Wherever your treasure is, there the desires of your heart will also be.

Matthew 6:19-21

I don't believe that this scripture is saying we shouldn't love anything here on Earth, but I do think it is telling us that we should be careful about what we "treasure". We should be cautious of putting too much emphasis on our possessions. Our biggest treasure should be our relationship with God.

Do you find that your material possessions give you goals and your only reason for living? Does your stuff affect how you feel about yourself and how you live your life?

I want you to know there is a bigger calling for your life than how many things you can collect! You are here to collect, but it is not things. It is wisdom, memories, character traits, ways to do God's work, love and so much more. None of which has anything to do with how many things are in your home.

What is in our heart and how we contribute to making the world a better place is what matters to God. After all, someday those possessions will be gone and at that point,, what will be left of your time here on Earth? How will people remember you? Trust me, my friend, you will not be remembered for how many pairs of shoes you owned (unless maybe if you are Jackie O)!

I have had the experience of emptying countless homes. Clients have hired me to do this for them when a loved one has passed away. I have also done this for both of my grandparents' homes. It is a crazy experience, to be honest with you. It can be very overwhelming. But each time I have done this the same thoughts go through my head: I imagine how many hours that person worked to obtain their possessions and how many hours they spent cleaning, rearranging, moving things in and out. And yet even though they gave so much of their lives to these things, here the stuff remains on Earth when they are gone. What is it all for? My sincere prayer is that it was all worth it and that these material items gave them joy while they lived with them. But in the end, we ALL leave here empty-handed.

I feel compelled to stop right here for a minute and say something you NEED TO HEAR, even though it may be hard. First of all, taking responsibility for most of your things before you go, is a gift you can give your children. If you have things, you can part with now, do not wait. If you are getting older and you have things you want your children to have when you are gone, and you can part with it now, do it! By passing these items on, you can experience the joy of giving! Stuff passed down from generation to generation is only memorable if you share the story behind it. Tell your kids about the time you all went on vacation and purchased that ornament. Organize those photos into a story that they can watch come to life. Explain how your grandfather worked to save up for that ring he gave your grandmother. If it is really important to you, tell your children why. And not in a guilt-induced way!

Speaking of guilt, if you have a history of guilting your children into taking your stuff, you need to stop now! I have seen this time and time again. In fact, I have a good friend of mine whose parents consistently drop items they no longer want at her house to "give her." She doesn't have the heart to tell them no, so she waits until they leave and right out to the curb it goes!

Why do parents do this? Because they have not learned to part with things themselves. They would rather have their kids take it than give it to a local non-profit that will put it into the hands of people that actually need these things! My advice? Ask once and if your kids decline, kindly say, "OK no problem!" After all, these are the things YOU bought. This doesn't mean your children will have the same taste or attachment to them and that is OK.

My point about taking responsibility for your stuff before you leave this Earth, as much as possible anyway, is also because it takes a tremendous amount of time and energy to clear out a deceased person's belongings. Your children will miss time from work, time with their spouse, and time with their children, to get the job done. So the more you can tackle your stuff now, the more time you will save them later. They will greatly appreciate this. Trust me!

> Let us strip off every weight that slows us down, especially the sin that so easily trips us up. And let us run with endurance the race God has set before us.
>
> Hebrews 12:1

- *Is your home a true external reflection of who you are on the inside?*
- *Does your mind feel as cluttered as your home looks?*
- *What are the things you own costing you?*

Have you ever realized that everything you own or bring into your home uses up some amount of space, time, energy, and/or money? Think about it. We only have so much S.T.E.M. in our life. I think it is super important that we become intentional with how we spend our S.T.E.M. The next time you feel the urge to buy a bigger house ask yourself:

- *Are you OK spending more time and energy cleaning a bigger house?*
- *Do you want to spend the money it costs to obtain and maintain a larger home?*

Are you willing to take away time, energy, and money from other areas of your life to own this type of home? Seriously, we are all so quick to look at the pros of getting what we want. But sometimes, we need to stop and consider the cons, too.

When we are constantly filling ourselves up with things, we

are less focused on filling up with God! Lasting joy does not come from stuff!

When we don't know who we are in Christ, we will try to find our identity in the things we own or what we have, such as our job, security, wardrobe, house, car, relationships, etc. We find real contentment, joy, and wealth by developing our spiritual life not by building a collection of possessions.

While I was reading Jen Hatmaker's book *Seven: An Experimental Mutiny Against Excess*, this statement by her got me thinking. Jen says, "Clothes used to define me when my genuine identity was fuzzy. When I didn't know who I was or what I was here for, I dressed like someone who did."[x] I wonder how many people can relate to this? Can you?

In Mark 10:21, Jesus tells a rich young man: "Go and sell all your possessions and give the money to the poor, and you will have treasure in heaven. Then come, follow me."

What would you say if God asked you to sell your possessions, but with a guarantee that you would spend eternity in Heaven with Him? Would you do it? The funny thing is that I don't think God even wants us to sell everything we own. But I do believe He wants us to have an open hand with all of it. I think He wants us to bless people with it whenever we can.

In this chapter, Jesus goes on to tell His disciples how hard it is for a rich man to enter the Kingdom:

"Dear children, it is very hard to enter the Kingdom of God. In fact, it is easier for a camel to go through the eye of a needle than for a rich person to enter the Kingdom of God!" (Mark 10: 24-25)

Does this mean just because you are rich you will have a harder time getting into Heaven? Absolutely not! Jesus is using this statement as a warning for those that have so much they become self-reliant. So often we don't seek God unless we are in desperate need of something. When we have abundance we start to think we can do this life on our own. However, a person who has everything here on Earth can still lack what is most important - eternal life.

Here are some ways you can take back control of your possessions and start being more intentional about what you allow in your home:

1. Ask yourself: Do I love this or do I use this?

Most people can add 20% more usable space to their home if they eliminate the stuff they no longer love or use. Sometimes we like the idea of owning things more than we use or love our things. For example, if you buy a lot of books, do you actually read them or do you get sucked in by the pretty cover and the idea of reading that book?

2. Remove the rest.

When you realize you no longer love or use something, remove it from your home as soon as possible. Consider selling it or donating it to a local charity that is close to your heart. We will get into these options more in the chapter about giving.

3. Be intentional about how you spend your S.T.E.M.

Consider why you would like more space, time, energy and money in your life. Get specific about what you would do with that additional S.T.E.M. Then walk around your home and decide what you could give up to gain more S.T.E.M. Next time you are about to make a purchase consider the S.T.E.M., it will cost you.

4. Never keep things out of guilt.

Just because someone gave you an item does not mean you have to keep it forever. I know this sounds a little crude to some of you, but your home should be a reflection of who you are, not other people.

What if you are not sure about what possessions to keep? As a professional organizer, it is not my job to tell my clients what they should and shouldn't keep. It is my job to help them figure out what they want their life to become. Then I guide them as to what stuff will serve that life and what is just getting in the way. There is not one list of things that is right or wrong for people. But being comfortable with removing stuff when it no longer serves you is crucial for living in a clean space and being happy.

There is a direct connection between the outer order and inner calm. If you don't believe me, stare at a cluttered area of your home for 10 minutes. Take note of how it makes you feel. You may feel stressed, overwhelmed, embarrassed, or tired. Then declutter and organize that space and stare at it for another 10 minutes.

Again, check in with your emotions. I guarantee that you now feel better than you did before. You now probably feel energized, happy, calm, or even giddy. THAT is the reason why it is so important to be intentional about your possessions!

"This is what the Lord of Heaven's Armies says: Look at what's happening to you! You have planted much but harvest little. You eat but are not satisfied, You drink but are still thirsty. You put on clothes but cannot keep warm; Your wages disappear as though you were putting them in pockets filled with holes!" (Haggai 1:5-6)

This scripture reminds me of what I like to call "The 5-Minute-High" principal. That feeling of joy or contentment you get when you purchase something. How many times have you gone into Target, bought something, and got in your car feeling elated? On your drive home, you can hardly wait to get that object into your house and put it somewhere! Oh, the joy you are feeling! You know this item will make you so happy!

Fast forward a month, six months, a year, maybe even more. Is that object still giving you joy every time you pass by it? Maybe, and if that is the case, you made a smart purchase! But ninety percent of the time, I would bet this is not the case. You may not even remember which items in your house made you feel that way to begin with!

Many times, our desire for more or better possessions is a longing to fill an empty place inside of us. In that scripture above, God uses Haggai to give a message to the people of Jerusalem because they were more worried about making their homes beautiful and gaining things, than they were about doing God's work of rebuilding the Temple. The harder they worked, the less they had, because they were ignoring their spiritual lives. The same will happen to us. We can work hard to gather more and more stuff, but without God, as the center of our life, we will never stay satisfied. We will always want more and more because true contentment only comes from a personal relationship with our creator.

How many times a week have you scrolled through Instagram or Facebook or through the pages of a magazine, wishing you had what other people have? We all do this to some point, but be careful that you are not coveting. To covet is to wish to have the possessions of others. It goes beyond admiring someone else's possessions or thinking "I would like to have that." Coveting includes envy -resenting the fact that others have what you don't have. In today's society, we see other people's possessions more than ever. Never before has it been so easy to see inside other people's home and lives. In fact, social influencers are encouraged to share as much as possible! If you find yourself secretly coveting the people you follow, it may be time to unfollow them or at least put the phone down.

As a professional organizer, I am privileged to be able to visit many homes and get an intimate view of the lives of my clients. Often I get to know these people so well that we become friends. They lean on me for guidance, accountability, systems, and resources. Many times I end up becoming their biggest cheerleader!

There have been countless times when I get a call from a new client that leads me to a beautiful home, with a perfectly manicured yard and a row of really nice cars in the driveway. I pull into the driveway and notice that on the outside anyone would think this person is living the "perfect American dream", only to meet an overwhelmed homeowner (usually a woman) when the front door opens.

Dina was one of these women. She had it all: three beautiful children, a huge gorgeous home in a high-end neighborhood, and married to a successful doctor. She was beautiful and extremely intelligent with a medical degree.

However, the woman that opened the door that day differed greatly from the one you might imagine with those credentials. She was overwhelmed, defeated and severely depressed. She was in the middle of a failing marriage, dealing with a child with special needs all alone, and currently unemployed. Her home was beautiful but a complete disaster and her inner spiritual life was in an abyss. My heart broke for Dina that first day, but I could see the possibilities for her life, and I was determined to help her make them her reality.

Dina and I have become close friends over the years. The person she is today still blows my mind. God has done "a good work" in her.

Dina tried everything to save her marriage. Unfortunately, in the end, she realized the abuse was just not worth it. Her husband was not going to change. She gave up her big house, along with most of her possessions, to start over. Not only did she go back to work as a pediatrician, but she has since realized her purpose in aligning pediatrics with supporting the needs of children's mental health. She is an advocate for pediatric mental health across the United States. Her children have grown into happy, healthy, successful young adults.

Dina eliminated the clutter of toxic relationships, stuff she did not love, excess weight, debt, and the opinions of others. After several years grieving the loss of her marriage and all that she thought her life was supposed to look like, I am happy to say she has also eliminated the clutter of regrets. Dina worked hard on herself, sought counseling, got organized, and spent many, many hours rebuilding her relationship with God.

This past year, Dina has finally realized her self worth and started dating again. I am thrilled to report that she is now in love with a Christ-centered man who appreciates her for who she is and what she stands for. Dina looks better than ever and is so much happier than the woman that opened the door that first day we met.

Dina is where she is today because she was willing to ask for help when she needed it. She was committed to growth. When she cleared the clutter that was distracting her, she realized that God had a specific purpose for her life.

Jesus taught that our loyalty should be to things that cannot fade, cannot be stolen or used up, and never wear out. We should not be fascinated with our possessions, lest they possess us. Without God in our life, everything will become useless, no matter how valuable it seems at first.

In Kris Vallotton's book: *Poverty, Riches and Wealth, Moving From A Life Of Lack into True Kingdom Abundance*, he reminds us that "Rich people get their identity from the things they own: their houses, cars, yachts, money, etc. Wealthy people's identity comes from who they are, not what they own."[xi] The main difference between "rich" people and "wealthy" people is their mindset.

God says A LOT about possessions in the Bible! God knows that material items will never make anyone happy for long. Only He can supply all of our needs. Idolatry is making anything more important than God. The people in the Old Testament were warned about worshiping idols. It might be hard for us to understand today why they were so enamored with idols made of stone and wood. But today, we are struggling with the same thing in a different way. Money, success, beauty, and possessions are the idols of today. Do we think these things can give us the same peace and joy that God provides?

I don't know about you, but these words in Leviticus excite me when God explains what will happen when we obey His commands: "I will look favorably upon you, making you fertile and multiplying your people. And I will fulfill my covenant with you. You will have such a surplus of crops that you will need to clear out the old grain to make room for the new harvest!" (Leviticus 26:9-10)

1. Spending Freeze.

If you want to get really radical, I recommend trying a spending freeze. A spending freeze means you stop buying possessions for awhile. It can be very helpful when you are working on getting your home organized. Initially, it will make your life easier because buying more adds to the work! Second, it will reboot your mind so you can start viewing your possessions differently. If you are feeling extra overwhelmed by clutter, the best thing you can do is get organized and reduce the number of items in your home.

2. Marketing Awareness.

On average we see about 5,000 marketing messages per day. The purpose of these messages is to get us to want more and think we need more. The people behind these messages know how to do this well. It is crucial that we become aware of how these messages affect us. Most of them are lies: we don't NEED more. Most products will not improve your life.

3. Practice Gratitude for Moments.

By now we have all heard about the benefits of practicing gratitude. But I want to encourage you to focus your gratitude on the moments in your life instead of the stuff. Be thankful for the memories you are making and the experiences you are blessed with. It will help train your mind to focus on <u>living</u> more than things.

CHAPTER 4: PREPARE

Be prepared. You're up against far more then you can handle on your own.
Ephesians 5:13 (The Message)

If you read the Bible, you will notice that preparation is part of God's nature and His plan. Throughout history, He has worked in the lives of people, nations, and circumstances to prepare individuals and groups for His opportunities, His purposes, and His blessings.

Preparing yourself for the dream God has given you is an act of faith. It shows God that you trust Him and have faith that whatever plans He has for you will come to pass. The very definition of prepare means "to make ready beforehand for some purpose, use or activity." There is that little word "purpose" again!

As I write this book, I am in the middle of preparing for the vision that God has given me for using my organizing platform for ministry. I believe the best work is written when someone documents their life lessons or experiences as they are living them. When God gave me the vision for a ministry in September 2017, I was a little caught off guard. Honestly, I had no idea how I was going to pull off such a large vision. But He began placing people, books, and messages in my life that helped me to see that this vision could come to pass with His help.

In May, friends started mentioning to me that Terri Savelle Foy had been discussing my book: *Organize Now!* on her television show and podcast. I was really excited because I had recently started following Terri in my quest to further my knowledge about declaring affirmations over my vision. I reached out to Terri, and after a series of animated emails, we planned to meet face to face at the Balanced Living Conference in Toronto. That weekend I learned the importance of preparation as an act of anticipation and how to act and speak about things that do not yet appear as though they have already happened. I thank you, Terri, for teaching me that one! Preparing for what God told you would come to pass shows faith and trust in Him.

A couple of days later I was listening to Cynthia Brazelton preach (I became a huge fan after hearing her speak at the conference). As God so often orchestrates, it was the exact message I needed to hear on that day. Cynthia spoke of the importance of making a decision and deciding that you are going to follow God and His purpose for your life, no matter what. Even if you don't know how you are going to pull it off, you need to say yes to God and trust Him. That day, I decided to pursue a life of ministry within my role as an organizing expert. Let me tell you that at that moment, I felt excited and scared to death. I said out loud, "OK God let's do this!"

There is so much you can do to prepare for your purpose. First, you can begin doing the inner work of strengthening your character. I truly believe that the essential part of any dream is not the moment you achieve it, but the person you become along the way.

God knows us better than we even know ourselves. After all, He created us!!! He knows the future which means He knows who we need to be to sustain the dream once it happens. For example, if you are going to put yourself out there in the public eye, you will face criticism. Not everyone will like you or agree with you (and that is OK). So God wants to build a tough skin, an open heart, and a boldness to stand firm in the storm of controversy. God will always build you up to be the person He needs you to be in order to do what He needs you to do.

You may wonder why you should prepare for something you don't even know will definitely happen. Preparation gets you ready for an opportunity. It frees up space and time in your life. It will limit your excuses for moving forward when the opportunities start knocking. You will know you are ready because you have prepared. God is currently giving you small opportunities to develop you for something more prominent in the future.

In John Maxwell's book, *Put Your Dream To The Test: 10 Questions To Help You See It and Seize It*, he writes that before you start doing big things you can still find contentment in doing the right things. No act of kindness is too small to be worth doing.[xii] He mentions this quote (which I love) from Saint Francis of Assisi: "Start doing what is necessary; then do what is possible; and suddenly, you are doing the impossible." Here are some simple steps you can take to start preparing for your dream:

1. Get your life in order.

Many people feel that not having a plan adds to the spontaneity and freedom of life. But when we plan wisely, we experience more joy, less stress, and calmness that enables us to show up more for God.

2. Speak your dream into existence.

Speaking about what you want to see in your life as if it has already happened is the key to manifestation. We release our faith with our words. Come up with a list of affirmations about your life and speak them out loud every single day. One of my favorite ways to do this is to make a list at the beginning of the new year that looks like this: "2019 Was The Best Year Of My Life Because...". Then I write down all the things that I want to happen as if they have already taken place such as " Purpose Over Possessions became a NY Times bestseller."

3. Protect your mind.

Fix your thoughts on what is true, and honorable, and right, and pure, and lovely, and admirable. Think about things that are excellent and worthy of praise.

Philippians 4:8

I am a true believer that our thoughts can bless or destroy our future. Our thoughts eventually become our reality. For example, you could have a fit body and be the perfect weight for your shape and your height. But if you told yourself every day that you were fat, you would eventually believe it and in time act like you were a fat person (hiding behind clothes that are too big, feeling insecure, etc.). Therefore it is crucial that you learn to control your mind by filling it with motivational and inspirational messages.

It is not easy to stay in the space of your dream when you can't yet see it. Trust me I know! You may have days when you don't feel like preparing for whatever reason. On those days, I have told myself this simple belief: "Why would God bother giving me a vision for my future that He would not see come to pass?" I also remind myself that His timing is not always the same as my timing. But man, we are impatient humans right?! And then I keep going, putting one foot in front of the other, taking steps of diligence, practicing stewardship, and being bold! If you have a tough day, call someone who will lift you up, email me at: organize@jenniferfordberry.com, or pray for the Holy Spirit to give you a fresh dose of energy and encouragement.

The biggest distraction when you are trying to stay on the right path is Satan. He does not want you to succeed if you are working with God! He will do whatever it takes to distract you. Do not be surprised if you begin clearing the physical clutter from your life and Satan distracts you with other tasks or interruptions he doesn't want you to be prepared. Why? Because when we are prepared, we are powerful!

Do your best to avoid laziness and idleness. It is essential to give yourself time for rest, leisure, and relaxation to maintain balance in your life. But too much is not what we were created for.

In 2 Thessalonians 3, Paul talks about the proper way of living. In it, he makes it very clear that we should make the most of our gifts and our time doing all we can do to provide for ourselves and our dependents. I love this because it reminds us that we as parents are to work hard. Our children are watching how we live. So many times I have heard clients say to me, "I don't know how to maintain an organized home because I was never taught this." I truly believe one of our goals as parents is to teach our children how to be responsible, hard-working, grateful people. How can we do that if we are not an example of this ourselves? The bottom line is, if you rest when you should be resting and work when you should be working, you are living life properly.

Do you remember earlier when I told you about Terri Savelle Foy talking about my book? Well, she had mentioned on her show how she used my book: *Organize Now! W Week-By-Week Guide To Simplify Your Space and Your Life* to prepare for the next step she was going to take. She talked about how she went room by room in her house and cleared away clutter she no longer needed. She prepared. Shortly after she left her father's ministry, she moved to a new city,

60

and started her very own ministry called Terri Savelle Foy Ministries in Rockwall, Texas.

My house is in excellent order. Everything has a home. I don't keep things I don't love or use etc. I have to have my house in order because I am easily distracted by clutter. I know that I don't do my best work if I am distracted. But I still wanted to do something that showed God I was serious about my decision. I wanted to prepare for my new vision of ministry by eliminating any clutter that might distract me. So I decided to remove everything in my office that would not aid me in creating this ministry or writing this book. A clean slate! I tossed old business ideas, research from previous books I've written, and presentations that did not align perfectly with the new vision.

I also prepared in other ways. I planted seeds. I tithed to other ministries I felt were working to grow God's kingdom. I spent a lot of time in the Word. I listened to podcasts every single day while I was getting ready for work and while I was in my car. I listened to others that were doing what I wanted to do. I read a LOT!

Here is the cool part my friends: the more I "prepared", the more real the vision seemed. The more vividly I could imagine my dreams coming true!

In Elizabeth Gilbert's book: *Big Magic: Creative Living Beyond Fear* she says; "You can clear out whatever obstacles are preventing you from living your most creative life, with the simple understanding that whatever is bad for you is probably also bad for your work. You can lay off the booze a bit in order to have a keener mind. You can nourish healthier relationships in order to keep yourself undistracted by self-invented emotional catastrophes."[xiii]

What are your top priorities right now? I love asking this question when I am speaking to an audience. There is always someone that rattles off priorities like a proud little robot: "Faith, family, work, health, and giving." Then I ask, "How are you living out these priorities each day?" Maybe half of the audience will raise their hand, (usually less), but most of the time I see their faces looking perplexed...Hmm, They are thinking about this question.

Knowing your priorities and living them are two very different things. Priorities aren't just what is important to you, they are the focus points of how you currently want to spend your time. The priorities you have presently may only last for six months. They may last for a year or five years. It just depends on your goals.

The truth is, many of us can easily rattle off our priorities. Sure, if you are a parent, your priorities will include your kids. If you are a spouse, they will (hopefully) include your spouse. If you are a Christian, they will include God. If you like to be healthy, they will include exercise.

But how often do you go on dates with your spouse? When was the last time you sat down quietly with God? How often do you make time to work out?

I encourage you to spend some time today thinking about the top priorities you want to LIVE. Your priorities should be closely related to the habits you want to form in your life. If you WANT a priority to be weight loss, then you are going to develop the habit of working out regularly.

Come up with 5-10 priorities to focus on for the next six

months to a year. Back to chapter 1, what does that vision for your life look like? The Bible says to make your vision clear and write it on paper. Here are some ideas to get your sparks flying:

- *Loose 40 pounds*
- *Start _____ business.*
- *Sponsor a child.*
- *Improve my relationship with _____.*
- *Read for _____ minutes per day.*
- *Exercise three days a week.*
- *Create a budget and live within it.*
- *Learn how to _____.*
- *Spend more quality time as a family by _____*

  _____.

- *Figure out my purpose.*
- *Wake up earlier and spend time in the Word.*

The list is endless! Post it where you will see it every day, especially when you are planning out your week! If you want to add power to this, pray over it every single day.

Honoring priorities often requires hard work, but the work is always rewarding because it produces a result you will love. Look closely at your priority list and come up with five action items you can begin doing this week to help you live your priorities. For example, if you want to spend more time together as a family, start a tradition of a weekly family fun night or make a commitment to eat dinner together every night around the table. You may need to give up some of your current activities to make more time for your priorities. That's OK! No one can do it all. Delegate your low-priority tasks whenever possible so you have time for what really matters to you.

Commit to continuing your personal and spiritual growth. This type of growth produces two results:

1) Your priorities will continue to improve and align with your true beliefs and principles as you discover what these beliefs and principles are.

2) You will be more aware of when you are not living your life in a way that honors your priorities and values.

CHAPTER 5: PLAN YOUR TIME

For everything, there is a season, a time for every activity under heaven. A time to be born and a time to die. A time to plant and a time to harvest.
Ecclesiastes 3:1-2

I have been married for 19 years, and we have two teenage children. *Purpose Over Possessions* is the 6th book I have written. I have spoken all over the country: on television shows, radio shows, podcasts, at conferences, women's groups, and at churches. I work one on one coaching clients about three days per week. I also own and operate a semi-annual family consignment event called "Mothertime Marketplace" where families sell their children's outgrown clutter for money. I recently launched a brand new ministry in which we run a Christian teen conference called "Blurry" and a women's conference called "Created Order".

Why am I telling you all of this? If I had not learned the

skill of successful time management, none of these things I just mentioned would be possible. Without making time to complete each task necessary to achieve the goal, these would still be dreams stuck in my soul. Truthfully, they could have ended up as "what-ifs."

Time is the one thing we were all given equally. Yes, given. God has given us this precious gift of time and to be honest, He has not guaranteed how long it will last. He has, however, given it reasonably and with intention. Twenty-four hours to be exact. You can't buy more, and you can't borrow more. It doesn't matter if you are rich or poor, old or young, educated or not, you still get the same....1,440 minutes each day to be exact. The cool thing is you can use this gift to create any life you want. I believe that the secret to successful time management is prioritizing, planning, and productivity.

Prioritizing must first start with a vision for your life. Like I mentioned earlier in this book, you must take time to imagine the possibilities for your life. That painted picture sets the tone for what you want your life to be. Based on that vision, you can set clear goals and aspirations. Once you have established your goals, you will have a clear idea of what your priorities need to be to reach these goals.

Planning is the part that utilizes that 24-hour period. Your schedule should always reflect your top priorities. For example, if your goal is to lose 15 pounds, your priorities must include exercise and healthy eating habits, or you will never reach the goal. To do this, you will need to make time to exercise and plan out your meals. In other words, you have to be INTENTIONAL. I am sure you have heard about the 80/20 rule but if not I will remind you. 80%

of the results you are trying to achieve will come from 20% of your actions. So when you sit down to plan out your day focus on the tasks that are going to get you to your end result faster.

Productivity.

So what does productivity really mean? When you look up this word you get a really scientific answer which personally does not get me excited. But since I am a HUGE Tony Robbins fan, I will give you his description: "It's getting the results you want with less time and effort. When you're trying to understand how to be productive, what you're really seeking is a way to achieve your goals while having time to spend on what matters". Being busy is not the same as being productive and it does not guarantee you will accomplish large goals and dreams. Productive people know how to get stuff done. They have a system and they work that system over and over. They know how to eliminate distractions and how to stay focused. They know the importance of completing projects in a timely manner so they can move on to the next goal.

In the Bible it says that to be productive for God, we must obey his teachings, resist temptation, actively serve and help others, and share our faith. Are you being productive for God? Are you staying on task with your bigger purpose, or are you letting the world distract you every 10 minutes?

If you are serious about living your purpose, you are going to need to get serious about planning out your time. Winging it will not work anymore. Trust me! As long as you are alive, you will have a "To Do List" and responsibilities, so you may as well learn the best practices for managing them. The sooner you do so, the sooner you will feel calmer and more in control when you wake up in the morning and start your day.

One key concept for getting organized is that everything you own needs a home. This concept also applies to your time management. Even more importantly for time is the fact that it requires one home: one place that you store your schedule and map out your days. It doesn't matter if you use a paper planner or the calendar on your phone as long as you are only maintaining one schedule for your life. If you are currently using one calendar for home and one for work, combine them. It is also crucial that your calendar be mobile and with you at all times. Otherwise, you will have to remember to write things down later. I don't know about you, but chances are I will get distracted and forget!

Currently, you may be seriously overwhelmed with all the things that you need to get done. It seems this generation has more to do than ever before! I don't know if this is indeed true, but it sure seems like it.

You may feel like you do not even have the time to sit down and plan out your week. But I am telling you that mindset will get you nowhere fast. We have to take back control of our time instead of letting others and circumstances control it for us. Not only will this help you feel better, it will empower you!

It is easy to make other priorities more important than spending time with God or doing His work. But God needs us to follow through and complete our purpose here. Don't make excuses. Set your heart on what is right and get it done. To be successful in living out your purpose, you can not confuse activity with productivity. In other words, you can be "busy" and not get much accomplished. We are all "busy", but how are you using your time to be productive?

A few years ago I made a HUGE change in my life. I went from a paper planner to my phone calendar!! I never thought I would do this because I genuinely LOVE paper planners-what organizer doesn't, right? Each year I looked forward to picking out just the right one for me. There was nothing more exciting than that fresh, clean slate when I opened it up. BUT, it was inconvenient when I forgot to bring it with me, and someone asked me about a date or tried to make an appointment with me. Plus, all those cross-outs and eraser marks were ugly!

I'll be honest! I wasn't sure if I could stick with it at first, but after a couple of months, I started loving it. Here are some benefits of moving to a digital calendar:

- *It is always with you.*
- *You can easily drag tasks and move them around.*
- *The same calendar can sync to your phone and your computer.*
- *You can go back on the same schedule and see when an event occurred a year ago (or more).*
- *You can set reoccurring tasks easily without writing all of them out.*
- *You can have a family category that syncs with your spouse and your children for events.*
- *You can color code! My calendar is color-coded by these categories:*

Blue = Berry family activities

Green = Jen's health (exercise, time with God, etc.)

Pink = My business (writing, organizing, clients, speaking, etc.)

Orange = Mothertime Marketplace (my consignment event business)

Color coding my schedule makes it easy to see if my life is in balance. One glance at my week will quickly show if I am missing a relevant category.

Read about any successful person living out their purpose, and you will see a common thread: efficient use of time. If you want to be successful at ANYTHING, you must learn how to manage your time efficiently. Your goals lead to your priorities, which drive your To Do list, which is married to your schedule.

Goals = Priorities + To Do List + Schedule

Are you pumped up to get really good at managing your time? I sure hope so! Here are some steps you can take to help you manage your time more efficiently.

Organize Your To Do List.

Think of your to-do list as a home for your brain dump: a home where you store all your tasks so that you don't forget to do them. The truth is, you will never get to the end of this list. As long as you are alive on this Earth, you will have things you need to do. And who knows, we may even need one in Heaven!

So, I want to encourage you to embrace your to-do list as a tool that will help you get the most out of the life you have been given here on Earth. After all, if you have things to do, then thank God for the breath you still have! I also highly recommend putting your to-do list into a digital format. If you write your to-dos on paper, it will get messy over time, and you will waste time rewriting it over and over. I use kanbanflow.com to keep my list organized and categorized.

Categorize.

Divide your to-dos up by category to keep you laser focused. For example, you might have a "personal" list and a "work" list. You might even have one for a specific project. Categorizing helps you stay focused when you set aside time to work on this part of your life. For example, if I carve out two hours to write this book, I want to pull up the list dedicated to this project and not get distracted by seeing personal to do's.

Prioritize.

By prioritizing your tasks, it helps you to discern what needs to be done first. Often people sit down and look at their to-do list and have no idea where to begin. If you prioritize, you can quickly see what needs your attention the most. I teach the A, B, C method to help prioritize tasks:

A = needs to get done this week

B = needs to get done this month

C = needs to get done whenever you have time

Plan Out Your Days.

Plan out your time as far as you can. The more intentional you are with your time, the more you can get done! Grab your calendar and mark down every appointment that is already scheduled such as work hours, kids' activities, exercise classes, school hours, travel booked, etc. Decide on a time and day when you will sit down and plan out the following week: for example, Fridays at 4 pm or Sunday afternoons at 2 pm. Block out this time and treat it just like you would if you had a set appointment with someone else. Sit down and plug in specific times to accomplish the "to do's" on your list.

Example: you see on your schedule that this Tuesday you have a 60-minute window between the time you get out of work and the time you need to be at your daughter's volleyball game. That would be a great time to get three errands done on your list. Then on your way home, you can make two important phone calls: one to the dentist to set up appointments and one to call that painter and see when he is available. Voila! Five tasks off your list! You are a rock star today!!

Routines.

I am sure you have heard it said before that "the secret to

your success is in your routine." Routines are formed by habits. If you don't like your routine then you need to change your habits. My advice is to fake it until you make it. What I mean is, come up with a routine that will help you live the way you want to live and then force yourself to live this way for a minimum of 21 days. It takes about 21 days to form a new habit. Sure, there will be plenty of days when you don't feel like living this way, but do it anyway so it becomes comfortable and normal for you. I promise it will be so worth it!

Accountability.

If you want to get serious about making the most of the time you have, you are going to need accountability. An exact time management system takes serious diligence and self-discipline. I recommend asking one or two people to keep you accountable to a time management system until it becomes second nature for you. I promise this system will not only give you more control over your life, but it will help you get to your purposeful destination faster. Ask a spouse, a friend or a coach to check in with you regularly. Permit them to give you a pep talk or a swift kick in the butt when you need it. I have done this with hundreds of my clients, and because of it, I have seen lives transformed from dreams and possibilities to real purpose with passion!

CHAPTER 6: PRACTICE STEWARDSHIP

*The earth is the Lord's, and everything in it. The world and all its
people belong to Him.*
Psalm 24:1

Unfortunately, most of us have only heard about stewardship during church services that are focusing on budgets and building programs. But stewardship goes so much further than that. The Bible says that we are to be stewards of this world. This means we are responsible for managing what God has given us. He has put so much into our hands! Most importantly, He has placed His trust in us.

The following article, written by Mike Richards, does a really great job of explaining the idea behind stewardship:

"A key to understanding the connection between faith and stuff lies in the distinction between being an owner and being a manager. The concept of ownership is rooted deeply in our culture and society. This is evident even in very young children as they grab a toy away from another child, hold it close and with great determination, yell the word, 'MINE.' We carry the right of ownership into adolescence and adulthood as we prioritize our time and finances to purchase more stuff. The reality of this blight on our society is never more prevalent than on Friday after Thanksgiving as we usher in the Christmas Season with 'Black Friday.' This ownership mentality is not corresponding to faith in Christ. Growing faith in Christ cannot take place separate from the material reality in which we live. The more we understand Jesus Christ as our Savior, the looser our grip will be on material possessions, or rather, the looser the grip material possessions will have on us."[xiv]

We need to allow God to move us from a mentality of ownership to one of management. Understanding material items from this new perspective changes everything. As I allow Christ to take His rightful place of ownership in my life, I not only sign over my spiritual life to Him but also the physical and material aspects of life. This means I move from being an owner to being a manager. As a manager or steward, I start to ask, "What does God want me to do with this?" and "How would He want me to treat this?". Instead of holding onto my stuff like a toddler, I look for ways to use, share, and invest the stuff that He has entrusted to me for His glory, for His purposes, for His Kingdom.

Stewardship to me is showing God that I am grateful for the things he has already given me by being responsible, capable and trustworthy with that which he puts into my hands. Being a good steward also shows God that I can handle more. Have you considered whether you are being a good steward in your life? Here are some questions that can get you thinking about the answer:

- *Are your clothes clean and put away or are they laying in a pile at the bottom of your closet?*
- *Do you manage your meals and grocery shopping efficiently or do you waste food every week by letting it go stale or rotten before you eat it?*
- *Are you having a hard time maintaining your small home while praying that God will bless you with a larger one?*
- *Do you keep that car you wanted clean or do you allow you and your family to eat in it, leave garbage in it, or rarely wash it?*
- *Why should God bless you with more if you aren't being a good steward with what he has currently given you??*

For we will all stand before God's judgment seat. It is written: " 'As surely as I live,' says the Lord, 'every knee will bow before me; every tongue will confess to God. So then, each of us will give an account of himself to God." (Romans 14:10-12)

As we stand at the end of our life facing God in Heaven, we will be asked to give an account for how we spent our time on earth. In that movement, He will not want to hear a list of excuses like:

"I didn't have the time to do this or take responsibility for that."
"I wasn't sure what I was supposed to do."

"My children and my spouse were distracting me too much."
"I didn't like it."

No, that surely won't cut it. God will merely want to know what we did with what He gave us. Did we complain about the work or did we practice gratitude? Did we love with all we had or did we hold long grudges? Were we lazy or did we work hard every day practicing stewardship?

These are the types of questions that come to mind when I think of the most important conversation I will ever have! If I live my life to the best of my ability, it would be unbelievably rewarding to hear something that goes like this:

Well done, my good and faithful servant. You have been faithful in handling this small amount, so now I will give you more responsibilities. Let's celebrate together.

Matthew 25:23

Can you imagine God saying these words to you? Personally, I can't fathom anything more exciting! The amount of satisfaction and pride I would feel would be exhilarating! When we think of all Christ has given up for us we should be able to give it our best shot here on Earth. After all, this life we have been given is a precious gift, one that should be treated with high intention and responsibility.

Work willingly at whatever you do, as though you were working for the Lord rather than for people. Remember that the Lord will give you an inheritance as your reward and that the Master you are serving is Christ.

Colossians 3: 23-24

If you believe for something start today by showing God that you are capable of handling more by taking care of what you already have. If you have been given a family, you are responsible for practicing stewardship and leading them well in the eyes of God.

If you have been given a home, you are responsible for keeping it clean, doing the repairs, and opening the doors to others in need. If you have been given money, God asks us to share a portion of it with others, save a portion and spend wisely.

Several years ago my husband and I studied *Financial Peace University* by Dave Ramsey.[xv] I love what Dave teaches. I highly encourage you to look up Dave's 7 Baby Steps for getting out of debt trust me, it works! If you apply the 80/10/10 principal to your money, you won't go wrong. Spend 80%, save 10% and give 10% away.

What if you are now feeling overwhelmed by the amount of stewardship needed, to feel more intentional, in your life? Now is a great time to go back to that vision you created for your life. Does your life look like that vision? Could you streamline the stuff in your life enough to enable you to become a better steward of what you own? Remember, stuff takes up S.T.E.M., so be intentional about what you keep.

When God blesses us with money, position, or things, we have to be careful not to use them to impress others but to bless others. When we use what we have been given to bless others, we will be given even more because we are showing God that we can be trusted with what we already have!

We also have to be very careful about complaining about the

responsibility that comes with something you prayed for. One of the most significant components of stewardship is gratitude. God loves to bless us. But He likes it even more when we are grateful for what we receive!

Several years ago, I was walking on the beach with an old friend whom I hadn't seen in many years. I had always considered this person a "spiritual mentor" and had learned so much from her when I was in my twenties. We were catching up and chatting about life. She was in the middle of a move and complaining about all the work it was to pack up the house they were currently living in and unpack the new house. She was in a terrible mood even though it was the first time we had been together in 10 years! I asked her why she was moving. She went on to explain that she and her husband had gotten into some financial trouble. She had prayed and asked God to help them get out of it. She was amazed when the perfect townhouse became available, and they sold their existing house for more than the selling price! That amount of money was exactly what they needed to get out of debt and relieve a lot of stress in their lives. At that moment, I stopped in my beach tracks and said: "Why are you complaining about the exact thing that you asked God to give you?" She looked confused at first. I said, "God was gracious enough to answer your prayers and now all you can do is complain that there is some work involved? Obviously, if you ask for a new house, you should expect to have to pack up and move!" At that moment, I learned a valuable lesson: sometimes we can become wiser than our mentors. My friend wasn't the only one that had complained about answered prayers. I had done it, too. But in that moment, God taught me to be aware of it. I am so thankful that God taught me this lesson and I hope it will be a reminder to you, as well.

You are the manager of all the things God has blessed you with. Now some of you may be thinking, "How did God bless me with this home? I worked hard and earned money to pay for it." But have you ever thought of it this way? The right home for your family went on the market at just the right time. God helped you get the job you needed to help pay for that home. Maybe he put the right people in your path or helped you stay calm during your interview.

Sometimes we miss all the ways God has helped us get to where we are today: the opportunities He has aligned for us, the people He put in our path, the grace God bestowed upon us at just the perfect time HIS perfect time, not our own. Sometimes I wish I could watch my life as a movie being played back so I could see all the things I have missed along the way.

Practicing stewardship is not always easy or convenient but it is imperative if we are to live on purpose. Here are some steps you can take to help you become a better steward:

Be Grateful For What You Have Now.

If you are not already doing so, I encourage you to look at all your belongings as a blessing from God. The Bible says everything happens in His perfect timing. This would mean that there are no coincidences. Stop right now and thank God for all the blessings he has given you. Look around and feel the gratitude! Say a prayer of thanks for the possessions you already have.

Don't Be Wasteful, Use Up What You Have.

As a professional organizer, I have witnessed a massive amount of over-consumption in many of the homes I have visited. It is common for me to see a large category of products such as makeup, books, clothes, foods, supplements, shoes and more! If you already have something in your home, you can comfortably live without buying more. I encourage you to start trying to use up what you have. Not only will you save on your grocery bill that month, you will also waste less.   Part of being a good steward is knowing what you have and when you need more.

Plan Your Financial Future.

Create a spreadsheet of all of your debts. Write down what you owe on each and a specific date for that debt to be paid. Then write down your goals for saving.   Pray and ask God to show you ways you can make money and save money. You can find one already set up on my website if you need help: https://jenniferfordberry. com/shop/debt-reduction-worksheet/

Sow seed.

I love Terri Savelle Foy's quote: "While we tend to be need-minded, God is seed-minded." When you are ready to get serious about increasing your finances, you will want to sow seeds. A "seed" or faith offering is money given in faith that God will multiply and return to the giver. I encourage you to do some research on the Universal Law of Wealth and the idea of sowing and reaping. The Bible goes into great detail on this topic.

> A man's harvest in life depends entirely upend the seeds that he sows.
>
> Galatians 6:7

In other words, you get as much or as little as you give. If you look at your possessions as blessings from God with the attitude that you are taking care of His property, then you will make what you have more available to others.

CHAPTER 7: PART WITH CLUTTER

For God has not given us a spirit of fear and timidity, but of power, love and self-discipline.
2 Timothy 1:7

Back in 2007 when I wrote my first book *Organize Now! A Week-by-Week Guide to Simplify Your Space and Your Life*, I knew that when people are overwhelmed by clutter, they are not in the right frame of mind to read a novel sized book to figure out what to do. They are desperate for answers, and they are thinking, "Someone, please tell me what to do, and I will do it!" They are feeling overwhelmed because they want to part with clutter, but they have no idea where to start or how they are going to make time to get it all done. That is why I wrote the first book in a step-by-step format. The fact that it is still selling well today tells me that a spelled out plan is exactly what people want.

First of all, I'll explain what clutter is. I like to say that clutter comes in all shapes and sizes. It can be many things: STUFF, baggage from relationships, disappointments, failures, debt, excess weight, that negative voice in your head, and so much more! Clutter can be anything that is not aiding you in living your best life, and it always costs you something.

In my book, *Organize Now! A Week-by-Week Guide to Simplify Your Space and Your Life*, I talk about the cost of clutter. Here is a short excerpt:

- *Clutter causes you to feel overwhelmed or depressed.*
- *Clutter robs you of your energy.*
- *Clutter steals 50 percent of your storage space.*
- *Clutter makes life harder. You have to look longer, travel farther, and dig deeper to find what you are looking for.*
- *Clutter takes longer to clean.*
- *Clutter costs you money. If you can't find what you need, you buy a replacement. Or you may be paying to store your clutter.*
- *Clutter makes it hard to think straight.*
- *Clutter may affect how you feel about yourself. You may be self-conscious or feel guilty about your clutter.*
- *Clutter can affect your relationships. For example, if you feel ashamed of your cluttered house, you may be less likely to invite friends and family for visits.*
- *Clutter takes away the peace and beauty of a home.*[xvi]

So why is it so crucial for us to part with clutter? I believe that "clutter" can rob you of the life you have always dreamed about. Satan can distract us with clutter to keep us from doing God's will! Don't believe me? How many times have you decided to get up early in the morning so that you could spend time with God only to get distracted by other tasks? Maybe your morning went something like this:

> You set the alarm so that you could wake up an hour earlier today. You get up and start making a cup of coffee. You notice the dishes in the sink, so you start loading the dishwasher while you wait for the coffee to finish. This leads to wiping off the messy countertop and dealing with a stack of papers. You finally sit down with your coffee and your Bible. You inhale deeply and begin to pray, but then you hear footsteps because the kids are already up. You think, "OK, I will get them out the door and then do my devotional." An hour later, you are hugging the kids' goodbye. OK, time for your devotional. But first, you are going to throw a load of laundry in so that it will be washing while you spend time with God. Then you decide to make the beds quickly because you can't concentrate on God with all this mess. The next thing you know it is lunch time, and you still haven't checked in with God.

Let us strip off every weight that slows us down, especially the sin that so easily trips us up. And let us run with endurance the race God has set before us.

Hebrews 12:1

Space Clutter

1. Do I love this? Do I use this? These are the two most crucial questions to ask yourself when getting your space organized. Your home is the one place in the entire universe that is just for you and the other people that live there. Why not make it the place that comforts you, inspires you and just plain makes you feel happy when you walk in the door? To do this, you must learn to be very intentional about what you bring in.

My suggestion is to break your home into small sections. Go through each section and ask yourself: what do I love? what do I use? When you are finished, remove the items you do not want immediately. You can give them away (more on this in Chapter 8) or you can sell them. God doesn't want us to be a slave to debt. One of the easiest and fastest ways you can start eliminating debt is to sell what you no longer love or use! I am the owner of a semi-annual children's consignment sale called "Mothertime Marketplace". I started the sale years ago because I saw the benefit for parents to recycle what their children have outgrown. I also knew it was an excellent way to earn money for what their children need next! I don't know about you, but making money always motivates me to part with my clutter. Every time my sale rolls around, I go through our house and make a pile of things that my kids have outgrown or that our family no longer needs. After, I take the money we earn and put it in their college funds. This way, I never feel guilty for selling the items that others have purchased for them as gifts. The original gift will keep on giving well into their future. Check out www.consignmentmommies.com for consignment sales near you.

2. The second step of getting your space organized is to group like items together. Many times you won't know exactly how much you have of one category unless you pull that category all together. For example if you are organizing paper, that means you need to pull paper from all areas of your home, including the nooks and crannies you have shoved it into such as drawers, baskets and cupboards. According to the article *The Big Picture: Decluttering Trends Report 2019* by Kristen McGrath: a home's main source of clutter comes from:[xvii]

- *Sentimental items – 26%*
- *Papers – 25%*
- *Clothing – 21%*
- *Toys/Leisure items – 15%*
- *Books – 7%*
- *Electronics – 3%*
- *Other – 2%*

3. The final step of any organization project is to make sure that <u>everything you own has a home</u>. Meaning all the similar things that you love or use are placed into a specific space in your home. You will know your home is 100% organized when every item in it has a designated spot. Yes, items will come out of those spots but when you are done using them you should be able to put them back quickly and easily. I will give you a tip: if you do not have room to give everything you own a home, you have TOO MUCH STUFF.

Mental Clutter

Mental clutter can take a toll on your life and your ability to reach your highest purpose. Some examples of mental clutter:

1. Negative self-talk such as, "My dreams will never come true." "I am stuck where I am." "Who am I to have a calling that big on my life?" "I am not skinny enough, rich enough, bold enough." "I need to make everyone happy."

2. Worry and fear. These culprits can keep us from making a change in our life or stepping out in faith toward a new goal. Satan loves to use fear to keep us from taking bold steps into what God has called us to do. He knows that it is easy to get us on the worry train! But when we start to get on board, we need to remind ourselves to place our trust in our creator.

3. Perfectionism. If you are waiting for the "perfect time" to do something, you will be waiting for your entire life. The time is now to make a change, end a relationship, start a business, follow your heart, or write a book. If not now, then when? My friend, there is never really a "perfect time". There will always be questions, doubts, and fears, but stepping out in spite of them is what stretches us and helps us to learn. I wrote my first book in between my kids' naps, cooking dinner and running a little consignment store. My son was a baby, and my daughter was a toddler! It was by no means the perfect time, and you have to know this: I had NO idea what I was doing! I just started writing and then whenever I had a spare ten minutes I would write some more (much like I am writing this book

now). By the way, this is my fifth book, and it is still not the "perfect" time! But if I were waiting for that, I would never have finished book #1.

4. Triggers. We all have "triggers" or ways that others can push our buttons. Triggers are usually birthed from thoughts -thoughts that we have carried around for a long time. Thoughts that actually have nothing to do with the trigger or the situation currently taking place, but more to do with our perception of the situation. Say you have a disagreement with someone you love and then it turns into a big issue in your relationship. Something the other person said or did triggered a reaction in you, but it doesn't stop there. Now both of you are not just dealing with this particular issue; deep down you are dealing with your pasts that contributed to the issue. Now you are fighting over something much bigger than the original disagreement. The thing we need to remember is this: do not let your triggers define your perception. Stick to the truth and the facts. Perception is the thief of many good relationships. It is so much better to sit down face to face and listen with an open heart. Be vulnerable! At least the truth comes out that way.

Relationship Clutter

Throughout my career, I have come to realize something interesting about myself. I don't have a hard time letting go of things, but I do have a tough time letting go of people. My attachment to people is something that God and I have been working on together. Over the past few years, as my walk with God has become more intense, there have been some relationships that have changed form in my life. I'll be honest; I fought this hard. I wanted to keep these people in my life forever. I tried everything: sit down talks, letters, cards, text messages, and even prayer. But I have come to some critical realizations. For example:

1. A relationship will not work unless both people are fully committed to it.

2. Some relationships only last for a reason or a season and then it is time to move on (and that's **OK**).

What exactly does relationship clutter look life? Somewhere there is probably a long list but here are some signs that you have relationship clutter in your life:

- *A relationship that continually makes you feel badly about yourself.*
- *You are playing small around certain people so that you don't make them feel insecure.*
- *You spend time with people that do not celebrate your accomplishments.*
- *You are in a relationship that sways you away from God more than it encourages you to press toward him.*

Are there relationships in your life that you care about more than God? Are there relationships taking up time that you could use for God? Time worrying about them? Time spent on their problems? Time stressing over them? Are you more persuaded by others beliefs and opinions instead of pursuing an intimate relationship with God? Our relationship with God is EXTREMELY PERSONAL! Even you and your best friend will not learn the same lessons from God at the same time.

Several years ago two girlfriends and I had a vision for a women's conference in our area. We brought it up to some other women in our church, and they decided to come on board. We formed a committee, and one of the female pastors joined and permitted us to hold the conference in our church building. The first year was amazing! It was indeed one of the best days of my life. I was so proud of the fact that women came from all backgrounds, religions, and levels of faith. The second year was equally as great. But by the third year, it felt like the church had taken ownership of the event., something that was never part of our vision. I knew God's original concept was for the conference to be an outreach that was not connected to one specific denomination or building. We wanted women to feel comfortable attending regardless of their home church or religion. We wanted them to come and meet Jesus and not feel judged. During that third conference, I felt strongly that we had allowed the flesh to take over a vision that God had placed in our hands. It no longer felt right. I spent weeks praying about what to do and finally knew the right thing to do was walk away. It was an uncomfortable conversation to have with our pastor, but I knew I needed to be obedient to His call and nobody else.

I know it can be challenging to begin the process of clearing away clutter. Whether you feel overwhelmed, don't want to spend the time or just can't let go of the stuff parting with clutter can be an emotional process. But please do not give up because it is challenging or time-consuming. The rewards will be well worth the effort I promise! I have seen countless people transform their lives and add happiness to it just by removing the clutter that is slowing them down. I also want to give you two pieces of advice while you are decluttering:

1. Do not keep things out of guilt. For example: if you donate the clothing of someone that has passed away, do not feel guilty. Let their memory live on by giving the clothes to someone that needs them today. You are in no way diminishing your love for that person or your memories of them.

2. Do not live in the "just in case" or the "what if". I have heard many people say they keep things because of a scenario they have decided <u>could</u> happen in future. For example: "I am going to keep this furniture in case we move to a bigger house and I have more room". Live in the home you have now. Don't worry about the "what if" of the next house.

I remember two distinct things about meeting my client (now friend) Laura many years ago. I walked into her home and the first thing she told me was that she loved being a mom. The second thing she told me was that she needed to learn how to organize her home because nobody ever taught her how to do it.

Laura grew up in a well known family that lived in a house packed with stuff. Her mother, Illene whom I also worked with, was addicted to what I like to call "the 5 Minute High" - the act of purchasing things you don't need in order to feel happiness. But many times after Illene returned home, those items would sit in a bag never be used.

Since the time I have known Laura, she has suffered the

loss of her only brother and her mother. Her father had already passed away before we met. These losses have left Laura, at age 42, with only a sister from her immediate family. Due to these deaths, she inherited her moms' belonging as well as many of her brother's things. Much of this was moved into her house. At first Laura felt like she needed to keep all of these things as a way of hanging onto the family that she loved so much. But it was a HUGE responsibility and it consumed much of Laura's space, time, and energy. During her time of grieving, it was important to let the things stay. But as Laura began to heal, she was able to see these items for what they were.

I am so proud of Laura. She has learned how to separate herself from her stuff. She has learned how to decipher which of her things add value to her life and which don't. Laura has worked on letting go of the guilt that she felt when parting with her family's possessions. She now knows that passing them on to others does not in any way diminish her love for her family or the memories she has. Her home is now cozy, clean, and manageable. This gives her more time to spend with her children and her husband, which is her #1 priority. Laura has learned the greatest lesson of her life: life is short and the time together is what truly matters much more than the collection of stuff.

Laura's family is very typical of the families I have worked with over the years. They have everything they could ever want yet they feel OVERWHELMED. The stuff does not bring them joy. The lack of space, time, and energy causes them stress, and after a while, the material things begin to suffocate them because there is just too much!

Decluttering is the process of deciding what is most important to you and then clearing away the less important. It can help you get down to what matters the most both physically and spiritually.

> Yes, true godliness with contentment is itself great wealth. After all, we brought nothing with us when we came into the world, and we can't take anything with us when we leave it.
>
> 1 Timothy 6: 6-7, Life Application Bible

Isn't that AMAZING! We know this, but we don't live this way! Why? Because we believe the lies this world tells us, and the lies that marketing companies get paid BIG money to get us to buy into: You NEED this. If you buy this, you will be more important, influential, skinnier, healthier, organized, more respected, and you will save time! We believe the "He Who Has The Most Toys Wins" mentality MORE then we believe what God tells us! Why is it that we can't take anything with us when we leave this Earth? I believe it is because it isn't ours to begin with. It all belongs to God. He wants us to leave it here for the next generation and the next after that.

The process of parting with clutter is not going to be an overnight event. It is a project that needs to be broken down into specific steps. My prayer for you is that you can enjoy this process and not get bogged down by the work. Many times people run out of steam quickly because they are trying to rush through it. But anything worth doing takes time, patience, and perseverance. You can do this!!! I believe in you, and I am excited for you to reap the benefits of getting your home in order. Here are some steps you can take to get started:

Create A Plan.

The first thing you need is an action plan. Writing out a plan and scheduling time in your planner for decluttering will help you feel in control again. Make a master list of the areas in your home that need decluttering. It will be easiest to go room by room.

Schedule Time To Declutter.

This process may take a while, so be OK with baby steps, focus on one area at a time, completing that one area before moving on to the next. After you make your list, I want you to schedule appointments in your planner for each task on the list. If you plan one hour, I suggest setting the alarm for yourself. When the alarm goes off, move onto something else and give yourself credit for completing the task at hand. Over time, these individual tasks will add up to be big projects completed!

Get Help.

If you are still finding it challenging to begin, ask for help. Maybe you have a friend or family member that is good at organizing. If not, hire a professional organizer. We are expert clutter cutters! I am part of a fantastic network of organizers called "Faithful

Organizers." To see if there is a professional organizer from this group in your area, go to www.faithfulorganizers.com.

If you need more advice about how to declutter pick up one of my books in the Organize Now! series. You can find them anywhere books are sold, including Amazon.com, and my website: www.jenniferfordberry.com.

- *Organize Now! A Week-by-Week Guide to Simplify Your Space and Your Life* (great for helping you organize each area of your home).

- *Organize Now! Think and Live Clutter-Free: A Week-by-Week Action Plan for a Happier Healthier Life* (great for helping you clear away any clutter that is affecting your body, mind, and spirit).

- *Organize Now! Your Money, Business & Career: A Week-by-Week Guide to Reach Your Goals* (great for organizing your business, finances, and goals).

Finally, get serious about clearing away any clutter that may be coming between you and God! This process will show Him that you are ready to be used by Him for more! And the next time you are walking through Target, tell yourself, "I have all I need and more!" Remember there is a HUGE industry called "Marketing" that has been trained to get into your head and make you think you NEED these things, but these things are not what will bring you lasting joy!

CHAPTER 8: PRIVILEDGED GIVING

Give, and you will receive. Your gift will return to you in full-pressed down, shaken together to make room for more, running over, and poured into your lap. The amount you give will determine the amount you get back.
Luke 6:38 (Life Application Bible)

This passage is CLEARLY telling us that if we have any more than we need of anything, we should give some away to someone who has a greater need. Now at first, you may feel a little clingy to your things. This stuff makes you happy, or makes you feel important, but by FAITH, we have to believe JESUS! He is not saying this to rob us or punish us; He is saying it to BLESS us with more. This is how He works, AMEN! I believe His Word is true: as I give, it will be given to me. Holy Spirit, please encourage us all to have the courage to give more than feels comfortable at first!

There is an abundance of "stuff" in this world going to waste. Whether it is going to a dumpster or sitting in your home, unused and unloved, it is being wasted if it is not in the hands of those who need it most!

If you are living in a situation where you have the ability to share your time, money, possessions, or resources, you are blessed to be able to practice privileged giving. According to Google's dictionary, the definition of privilege is "a special right, advantage, or immunity granted or available only to a particular person or group".

Here are some current statistics I found in my research that may make you think differently about how privileged you are:

- *844 million people lack basic drinking water access (more than 1 of every 10 people on the planet).*
- *Every day, more than 800 children under age 5 die from diarrhea attributed to poor water and sanitation.*
- *2.3 billion people live without access to basic sanitation.*
- *892 million people practice open defecation.*[xviii]

Still not sure you are blessed enough to give? Check out this fantastic tool: http://www.globalrichlist.com/. You can enter your location and annual net income, and it will tell you how you rank against every other person in the world. For example, if you live in the United States and your annual net income is $50,000.00 you're in the top 0.31% of the richest people in the world by income.

Since everything we possess comes directly or indirectly from God and ultimately belongs to Him, we should freely give a portion of it to Him and a part of it to those in need. We all need to do our share in taking care of others in this world.

In the 9th chapter of 2 Corinthians there is a great story about Paul. He is talking to the Corinthians about giving and I think he explains it beautifully:

> Remember this - a farmer who plants only a few seeds will get a small crop. But the one who plants generously will get a generous crop. You must each decide in your heart how much to give. And don't give reluctantly or in response to pressure. For God loves a person who gives cheerfully. And God will generously provide all you need. Then you will always have everything you need and plenty left over to share with others. As the Scriptures say: They share freely and give generously to the poor. Their good deeds will be remembered forever.
>
> 2 Corinthians 9: 6-9

For God is the one who provides seed for the farmer and then bread to eat. In the same way, He will provide and increase your resources and then produce a great harvest of generosity in you.

In the Bible, God asks us all to be joyful givers, just like He is. He says that a tithe is when you give 10 percent of your annual earnings, produce, or possessions.

Wealth and possessions mean nothing when it comes to getting into Heaven; this is only possible with God. The more you have, the more time, energy, and money it takes to take care of those possessions. If you want to make it easier to keep your home neat and tidy, the simplest thing you can do is give, give and give some more! Not only will be you be a blessing to others and yourself at the same time, you will be getting back some of your time, energy, and money.

How do we decide how much is right for us to give? I think 2 Corinthians 8:12 can help us answer this question: "Whatever you give is acceptable if you give it eagerly. And give according to what you have, not what you don't have." Paul then goes on to share several principles to follow:

1. *Each person should follow through on previous promises.*
2. *Each person should give as much as he or she is able.*
3. *Each person must make up his or her own mind how much to give.*
4. *Each person should give in proportion to what God has given him or her.*

If you feel like you don't have enough to give you are to give what you can. Giving is not just about the money. You can also give your time, your possessions, and your service.

The spirit in which we give is more important to God than the amount we give. God does not want you to give begrudgingly or with a bad attitude. He asks us to give because of our love for others, and for the joy of helping those in need. It is simply the right thing to do. Once you have given, let it go COMPLETELY! This doesn't mean secretly thinking, "What if I need this someday?"

He also does not want us to give and then brag about it. Have you ever known a person that continually talks about what they have done for others? It gets really old! You don't need to receive credit here on Earth. Your generous heart will be well rewarded in Heaven.

Be responsible with your giving. If you are in debt, God wants that debt paid off. He wants us to live without the bondage of worrying about money. So sell what you can, use the money toward debt, and then give away everything that is left.

> And this same God who takes care of me will supply all your needs from his glorious riches, which have been given to us in Christ Jesus.
>
> Philippians 4:19

We can trust that God will always meet our needs. If you are worried that you may need that outfit from 1999 when it comes back in style, you can trust that God will provide a similar or even better one in the future! Trust me!!

God wants us to have what we need to care for ourselves and our families without being a burden to others. However, we should be willing to GIVE if God asks us to. This keeps "things" from coming between God and us. It also enables us to use our God-given wealth for good.

To help you get into the spirit of giving think of this process as a form of ministry. God blessed you with things when you needed them. Now if you no longer love these things or use them, you have an opportunity to bless someone else that could use them! How cool is that? Focus on the joy of giving and being able to help others.

Declutter For Those In Need.

I have found that most people truly want to give and will give freely IF they know of someone who needs it. When I speak to audiences about decluttering, I am always shocked by how many times someone will raise their hand and ask me if I know of a place that accepts this or that. My response is always the same, and I am going to share it with you now.

If you want to declutter your home, find one or two non-profits in your community that need donations. Now I am not just talking about Goodwill or Salvation Army. Almost everybody has heard of those two. I'm talking about the "little guys" - all the other organizations in your community that are really in need of items. The exact same items that may be collecting dust in your closets or your basement at this very moment! I highly encourage you to take a few minutes right now to do a Google search and get to know a handful of these types of nonprofits. Choose the ones that pull at your heartstrings. Not only can you make a huge impact in your community, but this is also the best motivation for decluttering your home. Just think of it as your own personal ministry! Who knows, you may even end up getting more involved as you get to know the people who are working behind the organization's name.

*As of this writing we are actively adding non-profit organizations to the "Local Give Directory" on my website. Check it out: https://jenniferfordberry.com/local-give/. If you know of an organization that should be listed I would LOVE to hear about it. Please feel free to email me with its website link and city.

Sow Seeds.

"Do not be deceived: God cannot be mocked. A man reaps what he sows. Whoever sows to please their flesh, from the flesh will reap destruction; whoever sows to please the Spirit, from the Spirit will reap eternal life". Galatians 6: 7-8 (NLT)

When a farmer sows seed, he knows exactly why he is sowing the seed. He knows what that seed is supposed to produce. If you are wanting an answered prayer I encourage you to give to another person or organization to show God that you trust him to answer your prayer. When you give an offering, say a prayer first and believe for something specific. Then wait and see how God uses this seed.

Gift Experiences.

The next time a holiday rolls around give the gift of an experience. Do any of us really need more stuff in the house? What we need is more time together! I guarantee that the quality time you spend with someone will be remembered far longer than what you gave them for Christmas in 2005.

Increase Your Giving Capacity.

If we have the Holy Spirit inside of us, we will continually learn, grow and expand our spirit. As believers, we should want to grow in the mature use of all resources so our giving should expand as well. God can give you this desire and enable you to increase your capacity for giving. Do not miss the opportunity to grow as your walk with Him continues. You can start giving any amount and work up to a larger amount as you go.

CHAPTER 9: PROVIDE HOSPITALITY

Cheerfully share your home with those who need a meal or a place to stay. God has given each of you a gift from his great variety of spiritual gifts. Use them well to serve one another.
1 Peter 4:9,10

God calls us to hospitality. Hospitality is related to stewardship and giving. Opening your home to share it with others usually requires some cleaning up and preparation, which shows God that you are a good steward of your home and a generous person. On a side note, if you are dreaming of owning a more prominent home, the best way you can show God that you are ready is to treat your current home well and share it with others.

One day my girlfriend and I were sitting around chatting about the fact that hospitality has become a lost practice. We counted on our hand the number of people that regularly invited us into their home (besides each other), and our count was shockingly low!

Being a professional organizer has a stigma attached to it that I live in a "perfect home" where everything is color-coded, labeled and Pinterest perfect. People don't realize that just because I am an organized person doesn't mean that things never get messy! I cannot tell you how many times I have gone to a party or visited a friend's home for the first time and they have said, "I was so nervous you were coming, I ran around hiding all of our messes!" This makes me feel sad! I don't like it when people are embarrassed about their home. I hate that they think I may judge them (Trust me, When I am off the clock, your mess is the last thing I am looking at).

The truth is, we are all afraid of being judged when we invite others into our homes. Even me! When my husband and I first built our house, we gave, many tours to friends, family and even some curious strangers! I knew they wanted to see how I organized every little nook and cranny and I felt like it had to be perfect. I think judgment is one of the main reasons hospitality isn't as prevalent as it once was, along with the fact that we all seem ultra-busy! We are constantly bombarded with images of "perfect" homes on Instagram and Pinterest. We often forget that professionals stage these spaces for the promotion of a business. They are not a good representation of the average home and the typical busy family.

When a girlfriend comes over and admits to you that her marriage is in trouble or your neighbor pops in to catch up on what your kids have been doing, how do you react? Are you warm and welcoming, able to stop what you are doing? Or are you distracted and maybe even a little annoyed because you were not expecting visitors? Hospitality is defined as "the quality or disposition of receiving and treating guests and strangers in a warm, friendly, generous way."[xix]

> When God's people are in need, be ready to help them. Always be eager to practice hospitality.
>
> Romans 12:13

In the notes section, I found the following explanation about that verse, which I think is beautiful:

> Christian hospitality differs from social entertaining. Entertaining focuses on the host: the home must be spotless, the food well prepared, the host must appear relaxed and good-natured. Hospitality, by contrast, focuses on the guests' needs, such as a place to stay, nourishing food, a listening ear, or just acceptance. Hospitality can happen in a messy home. It can happen around a dinner table where the main dish is canned soup. It can even happen while the host and the guest are doing chores together![xx]

Hospitality can genuinely enrich the relationships in your life. It also allows you to be a leader and a server. During His public ministry, Jesus and His disciples depended entirely on the hospitality of others as they ministered from town to town.

Recently, I have heard many discussions regarding church

numbers and percentages. It seems our society is becoming less and less involved with their local churches. I have had this discussion with several people, and the consensus is that many of us need more from a church. I think what we are all in need of is more community. I am not talking about more social media, I am talking about REAL, sit down, face to face discussions where we share ourselves with someone else. Time when we open up, laugh, cry, or seek advice. Where have these authentic conversations gone? To text messages, Facebook and Snapchat? You can't connect with a soul on an electronic device like you can in a cozy kitchen over a cup of coffee or on a soft sofa in front of a fireplace! Those are the places where deep bonds are formed.

The easiest way to provide hospitality is to make your mansion your ministry. Many people think ministry is something that happens away from home through church activities such as teaching Sunday School, setting up for a church event, or going on a mission trip. However, you don't have to be associated with a religious organization to be in ministry. The word ministry actually means serving God and others. So if you are a believer, you have a ministry! How cool is that? You don't have to go to seminary or have a pulpit; you just need to serve and love. Here are some of my tips on making hospitality easier:

Don't Over Think It.

You don't have to be Martha Stewart to entertain. If you have hot coffee, hot tea, water, and some snacks on hand, you are golden. When you don't, please do not apologize! When you begin by saying, "Don't mind the dishes" or "Sorry, my house is a mess!" you are not making your guest feel comfortable. They will sense your insecurity, and it will make them feel badly for intruding.

Be Prepared.

You will be more comfortable when guests pop in or get invited over last minute if you are prepared. A few different types of drinks, bottled water, cheese and crackers, fresh fruit and nuts, are the perfect items to have on hand.

Don't hesitate to offer hospitality just because you are too tired, too busy, or not wealthy enough to entertain. Have you ever made up excuses for not being more hospitable? Have you heard your friends or family do this? Here are some common excuses:

Excuse: I am too busy. I have so much to do.
Truth: We are ALL busy, remember that To-Do list is never going to end. But when your life is over, it won't be the tasks that count. It will be the time spent with others and the impact you made on their lives that matters.

Excuse: My house isn't big enough.
Truth: You can always fit at least two other people in your space. Playing the comparison game is a recipe for disaster and another excuse.

Excuse: My house isn't clean enough or organized enough to have people over.

Truth: Generally, people don't care what your house looks like. They are just happy to get out of their own. If you are embarrassed about the cleanliness and lack of organization, do something about it. Planning a get together in your home is the perfect motivation to get your house in order.

Excuse: I can't afford to entertain.

Truth: You don't need much money. Coffee is cheap. Ask your guests to bring a snack to share to help offset the costs.

Excuse: I have social anxiety, or I am feeling too insecure lately.

Truth: If you are feeling anxiety, be honest and stick with one-on-one meetups. We all have things that make us feel insecure, and that is OK. A good friend will lift and encourage you when you are feeling down. It is the best medicine for insecurity.

Excuse: I want to reach out, but I am not sure how they will respond.

Truth: My friend, do not avoid sending an invitation because you are afraid to put yourself out there. I bet the other person is thinking the same thing. Be bold! If they do not want to put the effort in, you know this is not the type of friendship you need so, move on and invest in someone else.

I recently wrote a post on my blog about Galentine's Day. I

originally wanted to write about making time for friendship, but as I was doing the research, I found out that there is actually a "holiday" called Galentine's Day. Say what?? What is even more amazing is that I found out about this "holiday" the day before we're supposed to be celebrating it! (God is so good like that). For those of you that have never heard of this day, the date is February 13th. Here is a snippet from that blog post I wrote:

> Life is tough! You know that. And the only one that is going to get you and I mean REALLY get you is another woman. When that day comes, and you are crying on the floor because your marriage is on the rocks or you found out someone you love has cancer, you are going to need a friend. Maybe your teenager is going through something significant, and you have no idea how to handle it. You are going to need a girlfriend to give you a pep talk. There will be days when you need her to remind you that you are strong, capable, and loved.
>
> But having a relationship like that takes effort and time. And not just once or twice a year, I mean an intentional commitment to each other. Any good relationship takes this type of dedication and work. So how do we have relationships like this? We make time instead of making excuses.[xxi]

Hospitality can turn your home and property into a ministry for people in the name of Jesus! Everything we have belongs to God and can be used for His Glory. Your home is a gift. It is the one place in the entire universe that you get to create an environment unique to you and the people you share it with. Everything from the decor to the entryway to the photographs speaks about you and your family. It is a representation of you. So why not share that part of you with others? We need to make hospitality a priority if we are serious about it.

Not only are we called to be hospitable, we are asked to do it with a smile on our face. Inviting people over and then begrudgingly cleaning up and making some snacks is not what God is talking about!

I love how Donna Otto writes about this in her book: *Finding Your Purpose As A Mom: How to Build Your Home on Holy Ground*:

> Your home is holy ground. How you live in your most intimate spaces and with your closest relationships matters deeply for the kingdom of God. It's part of God's plan to change your life and then through you to change the world". She goes on to beautifully write, "It's part of our sinful nature to discount or underestimate or just not see what is simplest and most basic -closest to home, so to speak. It's human nature to value the exciting or dramatic or highly visible over the mundane and familiar, to want to

"save the world" while neglecting what is right under our noses. [xxii]

Here are some steps you can take to begin practicing hospitality more regularly.

Set A Date.

I have often asked a client to set a date on the calendar to host a gathering at their house as a deadline for getting their home in order. If you want to get motivated to clean up your mess, invite people over!

Let Go Of Perfectionism.

Most people will be so grateful for the invitation to come over and get away from the daily grind that they will never notice all the little things you see. They will just be ready to enjoy the time spent with you. Don't let the idea of a "perfect home" or a "perfect meal" stop you from entertaining. If you open your doors, I guarantee God will open your heart.

Focus On Making A Memory.

Inviting guests over to do an activity together is a fun way to make new memories. You could host a cooking class, a Bible study, a book club, or watch a movie with your friends. Choose any activity that you would like to do and then think of the people you know that would be interested in doing it with you.

CHAPTER 10: PARTNER WITH GOD

Put God in charge of your work and then what you asked for will take place.
Proverbs 16:3 (The Message)

G od gives us resources and opportunities to use for His work. When we use these gifts wisely, He will provide us with even more resources and opportunities that can be used for an even greater harvest.

You may be able to pull this "purpose" thing off by yourself, but can I give you a piece of advice? It would be a whole lot easier and a lot more fun if you partnered with God. What does that look like? Well, chances are the purpose you feel in your heart came straight from God and was placed there a long time ago. He gave it to you because he wants to make it come to fruition THROUGH you!

Repeat this prayer:

Lord, for that which I don't know, teach me For that which I don't have, give me. For that which I am not, make me. All for the glory of Heaven.

Amen

Friends I have to let you in on a really, REALLY, important part of this journey for you. In order to live out your purpose, you need to learn how to make God your partner in this process. Actually, scratch that. You may very well get to live your purpose without God. For example, if your purpose is to rescue abused dogs and find them safe homes you can absolutely find a way to do that on your own. But, without God as your partner, you most likely won't reach the highest and purest potential within your purpose. Why? Because only God really knows what you are capable of doing. You may not even realize it yet, and that gets me SUPER pumped up, because I cannot wait for you to find out, how much potential lies within you! I have accomplished some things without God, but trust me, they were never as good or lasted as long as the things I have accomplished with Him.

There is power with Jesus on your side. When you get to that self-realization moment in your life when you figure out what your purpose is, that is the perfect time to go to God and pray:

Lord, is this Your will? If not, then please show me what Your will for my life is. And if it is Lord, I ask you to come alongside me and show me the way. Teach me, Lord. I put my trust and hope in you. Please use me to make the world a better place.

In Jesus name, Amen.

As an entrepreneur, I have always been good at finding and encouraging people to be my partner in various projects or business ventures.

I have had several business partners. But last year a weird thing happened. God started taking each of my business partners out of my life. First, it was a business partner I had for 11 years. We had a good partnership and built a fantastic business, but suddenly her heart was no longer in it. She came to me and wanted to sell the company that we built together.

Around the same time, I was splitting off from the publisher I had been with for ten years and stepped down from a committee at church I was on. My podcast partner also informed me that she could not keep up with the work, so I would have to keep going without her. I am the type who always tries to understand "God's Why?", so I just kept praying for wisdom and understanding. At that time, one of my prayers in my journal went like this:

Dear Lord,

Why is all of this happening? Why is everything that I have known for the past decade or so changing? Why am I losing these partners? Is it because I am not trusting You to be my only partner? You have given me these gifts and visions; I need to trust You to help me use them for the world!! Even people at church were influencing my opinions of what You are doing in my life! Lord I only want to be directed by You!

In Jesus Name, Amen

Not too long after this prayer, the answer came: God is my partner; with Him ALL things are possible.

I said YES to God. I kept that business and bought out my partner. I will tell you that the first event alone was scary, but a fantastic success! I was calmer and less anxious then I had been in years! Why? Because I was committed to putting my trust in my new partner! I needed extra help, so my husband and children also stepped-up, which made it feel more like a family owned business. Another blessing!

I fought for all of my rights back on my published books and won! God even placed the perfect attorney in my lap to help me do it- a Christian man! Coincidence? I think not! Little did I know at the time that this same man would become one of the first board members for Jennifer Ford Berry Ministries.

God prompted me to launch my conference, "Created Order", and my daughter and her friends decided to start the "Blurry" conference for teens. One of the new Christian women I met introduced me to a company that could produce my podcast, which saved me loads of time. Yes, God had an even bigger, more miraculous plan in store for me and that was why all of this was happening!

To be led into a partnership with God, you have to spend time with him daily. Just as you would have to have meetings with other business partners, you have to make time in your schedule to meet with God. In this time, ask God to speak to you, give you wisdom, and lead you to the right decisions. Trust me - this works! It is in these "meetings" with God that my jumbled brain of ideas becomes bright with vision. It is also when I learn the most about God's ways of doing business, treating others, and accomplishing goals. He is my most exceptional mentor, and He wants to be yours, too!

God has given us each a set of gifts, but we need courage and self-discipline to use these gifts for His glory. When you begin to use these gifts, you will find that God will give you a supernatural power to accomplish anything He needs you to do. You can't do it alone, you need Him to do it through you. If you find that you are leaning only on yourself, you will not have the stamina to keep going. You need God's strength.

I also want to emphasize how important it is to take action and walk in faith. Show God you are serious about this purpose by putting yourself out there.

In 2017, I took on a vast vision and some lofty goals. I made up my mind that I was going to:

- *Write and publish my first ever Christian based book called Purpose Over Possessions.*
- *Start a 501C3 ministry called Jennifer Ford Berry Ministries.*
- *Launch the Blurry Conference for teens.*
- *Launch the Created Order Conference for women and teens.*
- *Continue running Mothertime Marketplace as the sole owner.*
- *Continue hosting The 29 Minute Mom podcast.*

The entire time I have been writing this book and working toward these goals, God has been working on me. Each day I seek Him, and each day He teaches me. He has stripped me of a lot of clutter, both business and personal, so that I can rely solely on Him.

I know that when this vision has ultimately come to pass it will only be because I have a God that loves me so much that He will walk beside me, pick me up when I am down, and chase after me when I lose hope. The last one gets me every time. *Reckless Love* has become the theme song for the *Blurry Conference* and each time I hear those words I get chills:

> Oh, the overwhelming, never-ending, reckless love of God
> Oh, it chases me down, fights 'til I'm found, leaves the ninety-nine
> I couldn't earn it, and I don't deserve it; still, You give Yourself away
> Oh, the overwhelming, never-ending, reckless love of God.
> xxiii

That is how much God loves us! If you ask God to be your partner in the quest to find and live out your purpose, I promise He will say yes! God wants us to realize our need for Him. He never intended for us to do life without Him. But we need to invite Him in because He would never intrude. So go ahead, ask, He's just waiting for the invite.

There will be days when you get impatient on this journey, feel frustrated or want to quit because you're tired and it's hard. Trust me! I have been there over and over again. But God's timing is perfect. (Personally, I have found it is easier to remember this after your dream comes true).

When my husband, Josh, and I were trying to get pregnant

with our second child, we thought it would be as simple as it was the first time:

Step 1: Decide to get pregnant.
Step 2: Try and get pregnant.
Step 3: Find out you are pregnant.
Step 4: Have a baby.

It worked perfectly with our daughter, so exactly two years later, when we wanted to have another child, I expected that it would occur the same way. Well, it started right. Steps 1-3 happened like clockwork, but that step 4 did not. We were devastated when I went in for an appointment, and the doctor told me I was going to have a miscarriage. We were told to go home and wait. I reminded myself that for centuries women endured miscarriages naturally and that I could handle it, but it was horrible.

Then came another series of steps which ended in an ultrasound technician informing me that our third baby was no longer alive. Another devastating blow. So heartbreaking, in fact, that Josh did not want us to try again. He did not want me to have to go through the same experience, but I was not ready to give up on our dream. So with a little trepidation and a LOT of prayers, we tried again. This time I found out that my body was low on progesterone.

I didn't know if our hearts could withstand another loss. Then one day I met a pharmacist that told me he believed a medicine called "Regland" could help me stay pregnant. That man does not know this, but he gave me the best gift ever…hope. Not only did we end up having another baby we were blessed to have a son this time. Josh and I had hoped for one boy and one girl since we dated in high school! The coolest part was Josh told me it was a boy! In the middle of my cesarean, he looked over that curtain during surgery (yes he is in law enforcement so he can handle stuff like this!) and saw that our baby was a boy. I will never forget the joy on Josh's face when he looked at me and said, "It's a boy!". I immediately started crying because I knew God had truly blessed us.

God knew His plan, and timing was perfect the entire time. He knew what was behind that curtain! Does it break my heart that we lost two babies? Absolutely! But I know God meant for me to be Bryceton Richard Berry's mom and if I had not gone through those heartbreaks, I would never know the joy of raising this cherished boy. As for our two other precious babies, I look forward to the day I can hold you both in my arms in Heaven!

In the midst of your journey ahead, you will want God to speak to you and guide you. Pray for wisdom and discernment. Hearing the voice of God can sometimes be super easy and other times hard and frustrating. One thing I have learned is that when God wants to get His point across, there is no denying His voice. When this happens, I am left in awe.

About two weeks before a scheduled mammogram test, I was working in my office on an average workday. All of sudden I heard a non-audible voice say, "Invite Kristi to your appointment." Kristi and I have been best friends since we were in the first grade and have gone through our entire lives together. Kristi had never had a mammogram before, so I just assumed God wanted her to have one. I immediately shot her a text and asked her. She responded quickly saying, "Yes, I have been meaning to make an appointment." Two weeks later, we were sitting in the doctor's office waiting for our results when the doctor called us in one at a time. First, it was me - all clear. Then it was Kristi - he said something didn't look quite right and she would now have to get another mammogram done. I sat in that waiting room and prayed. A few days later our worst fear was confirmed: breast cancer. The process that Kristi had to endure for the next two years was heartbreaking. The doctors told her that had she waited even one more month to have an exam, cancer would have spread past the point of treating it without chemotherapy and radiation. I am thrilled to say that today Kristi is now another breast cancer survivor. Thank you, Jesus!

Many people struggle with issues of identity, wondering who they really are and what they're supposed to be doing with their lives. But the more fully you know Jesus the better you can understand yourself and the meaning of your life. Here are some action steps to help you get serious about partnering with God to pursue your purpose:

Spend Time with God Daily.

Read the word, listen to worship music in your car. Jesus tells us in Mark 4:24, "Pay close attention to what you hear. The closer you listen, the more understanding you will be given -and you will receive even more. To those who listen to my teaching, more understanding will be given. But for those who are not listening, even what little understanding they have will be taken away from them."

Even if you have not spent much time with God up until this point in your life, you can choose to start today. You may be asking, "How do I do this or where do I start" and the answer is simple. Don't overthink it, just start with 15 minutes per day reading the Bible. I highly recommend one that is easy to understand! (I personally love the Life Application Bible or the Message Bible). You can pick one chapter and read it from beginning to end, you can look up a specific topic and follow the verses explaining it, or you can use a daily devotional. There is no right way or wrong way to spend time with Jesus; all He needs you to do is show up.

Work Backwards.

Go back to that vision of possibilities you wrote down at the beginning of this book and work backward.

- *In order for that to be your life, what has to happen?*
- *What kind of person do you have to be?*
- *What do you look like?*
- *How do you act?*
- *What do you practice daily?*
- *Make a list of everything you can think of and next to each thing write specific steps you can take to make that a reality.*

Enjoy The Process Of Chasing Your Dreams.

How many times have you reached a goal, celebrated for a short time, and then moved on to chase a new goal? Over and over, right? That is life! When you were in college, you couldn't wait to get married. When you were married, you couldn't wait to buy your first house. When you bought the house, you couldn't wait to have kids. When you started that career, there were tons of "next steps" you couldn't wait for.

The point is, life IS the process. It is the everyday baby steps to get where you want to go. It is the daily moments when you don't give up. Don't miss out on those moments because you are so focused on the end result because guess what, honey after this goal, there is always another. The process you will go through prepares you for the promise God gave you.

Always Be Grateful.

When you find your purpose, and you live it wholeheartedly, boldly, and without apology, great things will begin to happen. At that point, be careful not to push God out of your life in order to give yourself all of the credit. Do not become too proud or too busy with managing your success and wealth. Always remain focused on the One who provided you this opportunity and your abilities. It is God who gives us everything we have and who asks us to manage it for Him.

Persevere.

"You need to persevere so that when you have done the will of God, you will receive what He has promised." (Hebrews 10:36) Without perseverance, you might not receive the promise God has given you. Anyone can give up. That's easy. But it takes utter perseverance to keep pushing yourself day in and day out when your progress isn't obvious or when your perspective gets blocked.

Be Open and Honest with God.

God already knows everything about you. You cannot hide from Him. So let your guard down and be honest with Him when you are frustrated, sad, or upset. He knows every thought before you think it, every decision before you make it. Talk about your choices with Him and know that every right decision you make today can set you on a path to accomplish something significant.

Rest In God.

Finally, when you have done everything you know how to do and have not been lazy, when you have given it your all and are not sure what else you could do, rest in God. Remember, many dreams will not be accomplished alone. You are in need of help and that help comes from the most loving and powerful partner you could ever ask for.

CONCLUSION

As we wrap up this book, I am praying that you will be motivated to take action. Hopefully, by now you are recognizing what clutter is in your life and are ready to begin the process of letting it go. Maybe you are clear about your purpose, or perhaps you are still trying to figure it out. Either way, I want to be clear that the most critical step you can take now is to pray.

One of my all-time favorite, life-changing books is super tiny, yet super powerful. It is called *Prayer of Jabez: Breaking Through to the Blessed Life.*[xxiv] The entire book is based on a simple prayer in the Bible, 1 Chronicles 4: 9-10:

> Oh, that You would bless me indeed,
> and enlarge my territory,
> that Your hand would be with me,
> and that You would keep me from evil.

This tiniest of prayers can make a massive impact on your life. I believe it sums up most of what you need when you make a choice to live out your purpose with God.

In the book Bruce says:

> Whatever our gifts, education, or vocation might be, our
> calling is to do God's work on Earth. If you want, you
> can call it living out your faith for others. You can call it
> ministry. You can call it every Christian's day job. But
> whatever you call it, God is looking for people who want
> to do more of it, because sadly, most believers seem to
> shrink from living at this level of blessing and influence. [xxv]

How sad that we shrink from blessing! God's very nature is
to bless! It is Satan that tries to get us to believe we don't deserve it,
not God. Friend, I am here to tell you that God wants to bless you so
that you can be a blessing to others. He needs you to be a blessing.
There is a reason, and it is part of the plan for your life. Take a bold
step and start praying that little prayer of Jabez every single day and
see what happens.

Sit down with God and ask Him to partner with you on this
journey. Tell Him how much you need Him. Only God can send
you that supernatural power, the Holy Spirit, to fill you with courage,
motivation, energy, wisdom and all the other characteristics you are
going to need to change your life radically. I am not saying that this
journey will be easy, but I am positive it will be worth it. Your life
will be SO much fuller, more peaceful, and rewarding if you are free
of clutter, baggage and the things that don't matter in this life. Just
put your trust in the One that will guide you…He is just waiting for
you to ask!

It can be as simple as saying a prayer and asking God to

show you the way. Something like this:

Dear Lord,

Thank you for this journey I am embarking on with you. Thank you for showing me that I was living small even though there are endless possibilities for my life. Lord, I want to know you, and I want your will to be fulfilled in my life. Lord, please show me the way: guide and assist me every day. Help me to be a good steward of all the things you have blessed me with and help me to be a blessing to others. Lord, I can't do this without you. Please be my helper, my counselor, and my partner.

In Jesus name, Amen!

My friend, I am SO excited for you! I know you picked up this book and read it for a reason, because there are no coincidences in life. You wouldn't have gotten this far if something wasn't tugging at your heart. I believe that tugging is from God! I believe He wants to draw you closer to Him. He doesn't need you to be perfect or have it all figured out, He just needs you to be willing to follow Him. I love this passage in The Message Bible:

We look at his Son and see God's original purpose in everything created. For everything, absolutely everything, above and below, visible and invisible, rank after rank after rank of angels - everything got started in Him and found its purpose in Him. He was there before any of it came into existence and holds it all together right up to this moment.

Colossians 15-17

The best reason for you to pursue your purpose more than your possessions is because when you use your time and your gifts for God's ambitions, you will be filled with joy and be blessed tremendously. Others will see you and know that because of your love for God and His grace on your life, you have been transformed. Generosity proves that a person's heart has been changed. When you give to them, THEY will praise God for you. God will get the glory!!!

And then you can lay your head on the pillow at night and know that you are pleasing to God because you are doing your very best with what He has given you. Not only are you a good steward with a giving heart, but you can feel confident that you are fulfilling the destiny that God had planned for you long before you were even born.

Don't just take my word for it that God is who He says He is and does what He says He'll do. Get to know Jesus personally on your own! If there is any doubt in your mind, be honest with God. Pray and ask Him to show you the truth. Uncertainty can be a good thing. It leads to asking questions and questions produce answers. I believe that God can answer your questions and you will be changed by what He teaches you in your own life!

I have believed in God for as long as I can remember and I have no idea why! I cannot pinpoint one specific moment when I decided He was real; maybe it was during a message I heard at one of the several churches my mom took us to. If we missed a service time, my mom would take us to another church, declaring that "God doesn't care where we go." I have to agree with my mom.

Why would God care what building we go into to worship Him? He didn't establish all these churches, people did! Sometimes I wonder what God thinks of all this separation. My personal opinion is that there are too many walls dividing us. I'd have to imagine that God would love to see us tear some of those walls down and all come together in His name.

So go ahead, ask the questions, do your research, pray, GET INTO THE WORD! I wish I could tell you that I have always made time with God a priority in my life. Sure I have always loved him and spent time with Him, but until I made it a TOP PRIORITY) meaning that it was one of the top 10 most important things I spent my time on), I would not be writing this today. He has changed me, taught me, and helped me grow. I now realize how much I was missing. He doesn't want us just to show up on Sunday morning, sit in a pew, and half-heartedly listen. He wants a PERSONAL relationship with every one of us. He wants you to initiate it. All you have to do is ask, and God will accept your invitation! He is waiting for you. You don't have to have fancy words. You don't even have to believe 100%. All you have to do is open the door a crack and say something like:

> *God are you out there? If you are, please show me that you are real. I am asking you to come into my heart and my life and change me. I need you! I can't do this life without your help.* Then wait.

Things may not radically change overnight, but if you are genuine with that prayer, they will change. God will start showing you the right books, people, messages, music...anything that will begin speaking to your soul. So pay attention! If you really want to see a transformation, pray for God's will and purpose to happen in your life!

I remember the first time I got on my knees and prayed this. Boy, was I scared! I remember thinking, "What if I don't like God's will for my life?" That makes me laugh now, but I am telling you that at the time, I was a little scared of that prayer (even though my own plans were not working out so well)! Today, I have learned that His will is the BEST plan for me because He can see the bigger picture and I can't.

If you are already a believer, then I encourage you to go for it and take your faith to the next level. I can tell you from experience that the higher you go, the greater the view!

"Ask me and I will tell you remarkable secrets you do not know about things to come." (Jeremiah 33:3)

As you embark on this new way of living, keep your eyes wide open to the ways in which God will show up and encourage you. Parting with physical clutter will open up new space for blessings. Your tastes will begin to change. As you listen and read positive messages, you will no longer want to spend your time with negative people. You will notice God bringing new people into your life that are interested in growth, improving their lives, and making a difference! This will add more fuel to the fire of burning desires in your heart! Having lived this experience myself, I have to tell you, friend, I am SO excited for you!!! Up until this point, you may not have realized what you were missing - I know I didn't. But once you get a taste of a meaningful, purposeful life, nothing will ever satisfy you quite the same again!

If you stumble along the way and need a little encouragement, don't hesitate to look me up. I would love to hear about the decisions you make after reading this book or the ways you have changed. I would love to hear about your purpose! You can always find me at www.jenniferfordberry.com or on social media under @ jenniferfordberry.

My prayer for you is that you will have the discipline and the courage to complete this book and then go after your own purpose filled life! What you have experienced so far is only a glimpse because God is just getting started with you!

PURPOSE
Over
POSSESSIONS

DISCUSSION QUESTIONS

Chapter 1: Possibilities

1. What would you like to change about your life?

2. What were some of the dreams you had as a child?

3. If you could do ANYTHING with your life, what would it be?

4. What would you do if you knew you couldn't fail?

5. What do you want your home to feel like?

6. What do you want more of? What do you want less of?

Chapter 2: Purpose

1. What are you most passionate about?

2. What skills or gifts do you think God blessed you with?

3. What do you love to do?

4. How could you help other people?

5. How do you want to be remembered when you have left this Earth?

Chapter 3: Possessions

1. What are some of your favorite possessions and why?

2. When you think about the stuff in your home how do you feel do you feel overall?

3. Are you keeping anything out of guilt?

4. Do you feel like your home is an external reflection of who you are on the inside?

5. In what ways would you like more space in your life? Time?

6. Are you willing to commit to a spending freeze on certain categories?

Chapter 4: Prepare

1. What top five priorities do you want to focus on for the next 6 months?

2. What could you do to prepare for your dreams?

3. What projects would you like to complete?

4. Can you commit to spending more time with God so that can He can prepare your heart?

5. What are some things you can implement into your life to further your personal and spiritual growth?

Chapter 5: Plan Your Time

1. How are you currently keeping track of your schedule?

2. How would you like to improve your time management?

3. What does your morning routine look like?

4. How are you currently organizing your To Do List?

5. Is there someone in your life that could help keep you productive and accountable?

Chapter 6: Practice Stewardship

1. In what ways could you become a better steward of the things you own?

2. Can you remember a time when you may have complained about an answered prayer?

3. What are you most grateful for?

4. What can you do to improve your level of stewardship?

Chapter 7: Part with Clutter

1. What ares of your home need to be decluttered?

2. Do you find that you keep things because of the 'What If"?

3. What types of things are currently cluttering up your life?

4. Which of the 4 Mental Clutter areas have you experienced most?

5. Are you currently experiencing any relationship clutter in your life?

Chapter 8: Privileged Giving

1. What are your favorite local non-profit organizations to give to?

2. How would you feel if God asked you to give half of what you own?

3. What types of experiences could you gift to others this year?

4. What areas of your home could you go through in order to find items to give to someone in need?

Chapter 9: Provide Hospitality

1. Do you enjoy hospitality or do you struggle with it and why?

2. When was the last time you invited people into your home?

3. Which of the excuses listed in the book have you kept you from being more hospitable with your home?

4. What are your favorite tips for entertaining at home?

5. Can you commit right now to a date/time to host a gathering at your house? What kind would it be?

Chapter 10: Partner with God

1. Are you ready to pursue your God-given purpose?

2. What do you think your God-given purpose is?

3. How often do you spend time with God? Would you like to increase your time spent with Him?

4. What are some of the beliefs you are currently struggling with?

5. What do you need prayer for?

FOOTNOTES

i Marsha Sinetar, *Do What You Love, The Money Will Follow: Discovering Your Right Livelihood* (New York: Dell Publishing, 1987).

ii Kris Vallotton , *Poverty, Riches and Wealth: Moving From A Life Of Lack Into True Kingdom Abundance* (Minnesota: Chosen Books, 2018).

iii https://www.thesaurus.com/browse/possibility

iv Jennie Allen, *Nothing To Prove: Why We Can Stop Trying So Hard* (New York: Waterbrook, 2017).

v Mark 9:24 (NLT)

vi Caroline Leaf, *Switch On Your Brain: The Key to Peak Happiness, Thinking, and Health* (Michigan: Baker Books, 2013).

vii John Maxwell, *Put Your Dream To The Test: 10 Questions To Help You See It and Seize It* (Tennessee: Thomas Nelson, 2011).

viii John Maxwell, *Put Your Dream To The Test: 10 Questions To Help You See It and Seize It* (Tennessee: Thomas Nelson, 2011).

ix The 29 Minute Mom podcast: https://jenniferfordberry.com/the29minutemom/

x Jen Hatmaker, *Seven: An Experimental Mutiny Against Excess* (Texa :Hatmaker Partners LLC, 2017).

xi Kris Vallotton , *Poverty, Riches and Wealth: Moving From A Life Of Lack Into True Kingdom Abundance* (Minnesota: Chosen Books, 2018).

xii John Maxwell, *Put Your Dream To The Test: 10 Questions To Help You See It and Seize It* (Tennessee: Thomas Nelson, 2011).

xiii Elizabeth Gilbert, *Big Magic: Creative Living Beyond Fear* (New York: Riverhead Books, 2015).

xiv Mike Richards, *Stuffology: The study of "Stuff" and how our faith affects our perception and handling of it,* (https://www.cross-point.org/content.cfm?page_content=blogs_include.cfm&friendly_name=stewardship, 2016).

xv Dave Ramsey, *Financial Peace University* (https://www.daveramsey.com/store/product/financial-peace-university-class?gclid=EAIaIQobChMInOvplpHf4gIVD7bACh3p5Qb4EAAYASAAEg-LRCPD_BwE#in-progress=1).

xvi Jennifer Ford Berry, *Organize Now: A Week-by-Week Guide to Simplify Your Space and Your Life* (Ohio: Betterway Books, 2010).

xvii Kristen McGrath, The Big Picture: Decluttering Trends Report (https://www.offers.com/blog/post/big-picture-decluttering-survey/, 2019.

xviii https://www.worldvision.org/clean-water-news-stories/global-water-crisis-facts

xix Dictionary.Com

xx Life Application Bible, notes section for Romans 12:13

xxi Jennifer Ford Berry, (https://jenniferfordberry.com/galentines-day-are-you-too-busy-for-yourgirlfriends/, 2019).

xxii Donna Otto, *Finding Your Purpose As A Mom: How to Build Your Home on Holy Ground* (Oregon: Harvest House, 2004).

xxiii Cory Asbury, *Reckless Love*

xxiv Bruce Wilkinson, *Prayer of Jabez: Breaking Through to the Blessed Life* (Oregon: Multnomah, 2000).

xxv Bruce Wilkinson, *Prayer of Jabez: Breaking Through to the Blessed Life* (Oregon: Multnomah, 2000).

ABOUT THE AUTHOR

JENNIFER FORD BERRY is the best selling author of the series: Organize Now! She is an expert at helping people get their entire life organized so that they can live out their God-given purpose. She is passionate about speaking to audiences all over the world. This includes hosting *The 29 Minute Mom* podcast and the *Created Order Conference*. Jennifer is the proud mom of two children and currently resides with them and her husband in Western New York.

CONNECT ONLINE

 @jenniferfordberry

JenniferFordBerry.com

THE 29 MINUTE
MOM

BECAUSE WE KNOW EVERY MINUTE COUNTS!

The podcast that provides moms education, inspiration & motivation in 29 minutes or less.

With Host:

JENNIFER FORD BERRY

SUBSCRIBE NOW

Jennifer is the host of *The 29 Minute Mom podcast.* The show's mission is to offer inspiration, motivation, and education to help you live your best life in 29 minutes or less.

Subscribe today on your favorite podcast platform and never miss an episode or find all episodes at: jenniferfordberry.com/the29minutemom. Better yet, leave a review and Jennifer will read it live on the air!

AVAILABLE ON ITUNES AND SPOTIFY!

NEW REVISED EDITIONS!

ORGANIZE NOW!
VOLUME I:
Simplify Your Space + Life

GET ORGANIZED FAST!

Clutter has a cost. It steals your storage space, robs your time and energy, and takes away the peace and beauty of your home. Don't pay for it another minute—get organized, now! This updated and expanded edition of the bestselling *Organize Now!* features even more quick, effective organizing ideas. Easy-to-follow checklists show you how to organize any part of your life in less than one week. You spend more time organizing and less time reading—a perfect fit for your busy lifestyle! Long-term goals help keep the clutter away for the months and years to follow so that you can maintain the order you create. You'll find help with everything from time management and routines to mental clutter, paperwork, pets, purses, toys, rooms and life events such as moving and celebrating the holidays. Special money saving tips show you how to use your organizing efforts to cut costs around the house and even make a little money. Don't let piles of paperwork, overflowing closets, and overbooked schedules drain your resources and energy anymore. Take control with *Organize Now!*

ORDER YOUR COPY

VOLUME II
A week-by-week action plan
for a healthier, happier life

JENNIFER FORD BERRY

ORGANIZE NOW!
VOLUME II:
Think + Live Clutter Free

FIND YOUR FOCUS!

You are bombarded with mental clutter every day—countless distractions, endless options, the perpetual to-do list—and it's holding you back. In this book, organizing expert and best-selling author Jennifer Ford Berry shows you how to quickly cut out the clutter so you can create the home you've always wanted. Shed the meaningless distractions to make room for the things that matter the most to you. Inside you'll find: • easy-to-follow checklists that give you results in just one week • lists of what to do monthly, seasonally, and annually so you can stay organized • strategies for making more time for family, friends, and your own well-being • quick decluttering tips to organize bedrooms, bathrooms, closets and more • help identifying and honoring your key priorities Learn how to focus your thoughts, choices, and actions to create the life of your dreams.

ORDER YOUR COPY
JENNIFERFORDBERRY.COM OR AMAZON

Printed in the USA
CPSIA information can be obtained
at www.ICGtesting.com
LVHW051830290224
772930LV00020B/1481